Advanced Praise for Hear the Music

Nathaniel Ayers studied string bass with me at the Cleveland Music School Settlement and was one of the most gifted and talented students that I had the pleasure of teaching. He loved music, was focused, and was very talented. I had felt that given time, he would be in one of the major symphony orchestras.

After high school, he received a scholarship to and attended Ohio University. He was doing very well, but since I had attended Juilliard in New York on scholarship, Nathaniel said, "I want to go to Juilliard" and soon received a scholarship from them. He went to Juilliard and was well on his way to realizing his dreams. It was with great sadness I realized his dreams would not become a reality after he called me from the hospital.

Fortunately, Nathaniel has a very loving, caring sister named Jennifer who has been his support system. After the discovery of Nathaniel living out of a shopping cart in front of Disney Hall in L.A. by Steve Lopez, writer for the L.A. Times and author of *The Soloist: A Lost Dream, An Unlikely Friendship, and the Redemptive Power of Music,* and the making of the movie, *The Soloist*, starring Jamie Foxx and Robert Downey Jr., Jennifer was able to create a foundation to help other people like Nathaniel.

In her book, *Hear the Music: Memoirs from the Sister of The Soloist*, Jennifer shares some of the most personal information about their early childhood, difficult upbringing, difficulties with Nathaniel being schizophrenic, and what they have gone through. This book is a guide for people who have loved ones who are dealing with mental illness and experiencing some of the same difficulties.

Harry J. Barnoff
Teacher, Cleveland Music Settlement, Retired
Principal Bassist, Cleveland Orchestra, Retired
Double Bass, US 6th Army WWII, Retired

Wow! "Hear the Music" is an honest and heartfelt journey expressed by Jennifer Ayers-Moore about growing up in a family where her brother's (Nathaniel Ayers, a.k.a. The Soloist) mental health issues were experienced differently by everyone in the family and their friends. Lessons are taught via musical expression and learned through love, understanding, awareness of the struggles, and advocacy.

 This is a beautifully written book that will help so many people start to voice the music of life that they hear – a great big one being Schizophrenia, which is sometimes simple and sometimes very complicated. This brother and sister have come so far, and Jennifer shares the most important ingredient of their growth: Never. Give. Up. It is an honor to be a part of this work to support those we love and care about the most, and the journey to create better mental health systems for them. Thank you for writing this important, powerful, musical metaphor that helps bridge the gap between love for and understanding of those who navigate the world differently.

Helen Dolas, M.S. MT-BC
Founder/CEO
Able ARTS Work

 Mental illness is a rollercoaster ride for millions of families – one day a struggle, another day a triumph. Jennifer shares from her heart the struggles and triumphs and endears us to her family in a way that leaves us feeling comforted and inspired. Reading this book would help any family dealing with mental illness.

Rebecca Phillips
Mental Health Advocate
Author and Speaker

Claire Phillips
Mental Health Advocate
Speaker and Rebecca's Mother

Jennifer Ayers-Moore writes an honest look at her years growing up with her brother, Nathaniel, as she allows herself to reflect on the effects of his mental illness. Her candid moments of reflection and then of growth, as well as sharing her deepest hurts through the eyes of forgiveness, inspires even those who are not currently loving someone with a mental illness to reach for and believe in more, to love, to never give up, and to ask for help.

BBB

Hear the Music

Hear the Music:
Memoirs from the Sister of the Soloist

Jennifer Ayers-Moore

Copyright © 2020 by Jennifer Ayers-Moore

All rights reserved. No portion of this book may be reproduced, stored in a retrieval system, or transmitted in any form, except for brief quotations in critical reviews or articles, without prior written permission of the publisher and author. This includes electronic, mechanical, photocopy, recording, scanning, or other means.

Published in the United States of America.

ISBN: 979-8-565-87791-5

Cover Design: Sheer Design

This is a memoir. It reflects several handwritten and electronic journals written by the author, depicting the author's life experiences, over the course of several years. All events and stories are truthful and based on the author's perception at the time of recording them in the journals and are depicted to the best of the author's recollection. Details of some events and chronology have been slightly modified to enhance readability and to ensure privacy while maintaining integrity of the truth. Some individuals have given permission to use their names. Some names have been changed or omitted. Some named individuals are deceased. Some notable names are used, because their highly visible and public work with characters and events recollected in this memoir are of great public interest. Any resemblance of any other party is purely coincidental.

Dedicated to the late Floria Boone.

Your light, legacy, and servant's heart lives on, flourishing in the lives of those individuals and families you touched. We may never know, this side of heaven, the impact you had on them, but I know the impact you had on me.

The dream lives on.
Thank you, Mom.
I love you.

Foreword

Jennifer Ayers-Moore's book, *Hear the Music: Memoirs from the Sister of The Soloist*, is a compelling account of her experiences with her brother, Nathaniel Ayers, from when they were younger in the wake of Nathaniel's diagnosis; and her brother being thrust into the public eye as a result of stories and a book written about him by journalist, Steve Lopez, which led to a movie also being made about him, called *The Soloist*.

Nathaniel Ayers is a gifted musician, from a young age. He started playing the double bass in middle school, and his talent being evident, was quickly referred to The Cleveland Music Settlement where he studied under Harry Barnoff. Nathaniel attended The Juilliard School, on scholarship, in 1970 at 19 years old. Within 2 years of attending Juilliard, Nathaniel began to decompensate into schizophrenia.

When Nathaniel started to decompensate, Jennifer and her family, at first, did not recognize what was going on. This is not uncommon in families of persons with mental illness. Part of the reason for this is, likely, that they do not want to accept something so painful. Another reason is lack of basic literacy around mental illness, what it looks like, and how to address it.

Indeed, we teach junior and senior high school students driver's ed, sex ed, and illness ed. Why not teach mental health ed, so people can identify what is happening when they or a loved one is becoming symptomatic; and what they can do in response?

That said, the best way to reduce stigma is not for people to see mental health disorders as physical disorders, but to put a human face on the illness. Jennifer's tenacious support of the mental health community continues to help end stigma by showing that those diagnosed with mental illness are humans who continue to have hopes and dreams. And the stories, book, and movie about Nathaniel helped put a human face on mental illness with widespread effect.

Steve Lopez had found Nathaniel on the street playing a defective instrument (a violin that did not have all its strings but making beautiful music, nevertheless). Steve was able to help Nathaniel turn his life around so that he is now living in a stable environment, is getting the care he needs, and is still playing his instruments with great passion and joy.

But there is often another feature of mental illness—namely its effects on loved ones. They include feeling pain at the suffering of a loved one; feeling anger when the loved one does not seek or want help; feeling fear at what might happen to the loved one; and sometimes, fear that they may become violent. (Actually, the idea that people with mental illness are violent is simply not true. But most people do not know this.)

Families may also feel shame that their loved one has mental illness. And they may feel that they are at fault or that others will see them in this way. The reality is that most mental illness is a no-fault brain disease and families are not responsible for their loved ones' illness. But again, many people do not know this, either.

The effects can be very complicated for families and caregivers and Jennifer does a good job teasing out these effects as she tells the story of her own ride as a close sister of Nathaniel. She helped him socially, and recognizing how gifted he was musically, Jennifer supported him in his musical endeavors, as they grew up.

Nathaniel enjoyed talking, so Jennifer shared many conversations with him even if she did not always understand him. He loved sharing his music, too, so Jennifer arranged for him to play at small venues, churches, and sometimes, she would simply listen to him play for her through the phone.

Jennifer being in Nathaniel's life during many difficult times shows her kindness and caring. It also shows her strength. She did not let this trauma knock her down or out of the race. She never gave up. She was always there.

Still, it was not easy. Jennifer missed out on many things because of Nathaniel's illness: having a brother she could both support and get support from; having a shared family history that could create a bond between them; and having worries about Nathaniel's health that could bear on her own family's health (stress can cause or exacerbate illness).

Of course, her brother's later success with the help of Steve Lopez gave her great delight and gratification. She maintained her hope through many years, and it has actually come true—Nathaniel can have a good and happy life in spite of his mental illness and mostly because of the power of relationships to hold him together.

There are any number of first-person accounts of mental illness. There are very few by people who are close relatives of someone with a major mental illness. The only other one I know is Jay Neugeboren's, *Imagining Robert*, about his brother's serious bipolar disorder. Jay tells a moving and compassionate story, and Jennifer's is equally as compelling.

I would recommend that anyone with a loved one with mental illness read this book. Indeed, it is really a "must-read."

Finally, I would like to thank Jennifer Ayers-Moore for her bravery in writing this book and her willingness to expose some hard things for the sake of helping others.

Thank you, Jennifer. As we say here at USC: "Fight On!"

Elyn R. Saks, J.D., Ph.D.

Orrin B. Evans Distinguished Professor of Law, Psychology, Psychiatry, and the Behavioral Sciences
University of Southern California Gould School of Law

Adjunct Professor of Psychiatry
University of California, San Diego, School of Medicine

Director
Saks Institute for Mental Health Law, Policy, and Ethics

Faculty
New Center for Psychoanalysis

Prelude

One could look at my life and see that it was much like too many others' – a two-time child of divorce; suffered from health issues; a witness to racism; a divorcee; a single, adoptive mother; abandoned and all but forgotten by my absentee father. The way it differs, however, is that my brother – once a promising, double bassist who attended The Juilliard School on scholarship in the 1970s – was diagnosed with schizophrenia and, eventually, ended up homeless on Skid Row in L.A. He was discovered by an L.A. journalist who wrote a book about him that was made into a mainstream, Hollywood movie.

You can read all about this aspect of my brother's life by doing a quick web search. You will even come across interviews with me giving "the real, behind-the-scenes scoop" about my brother and his life. But the things you read or see in the movie about my brother and me are only small snippets of our story. While I am grateful that these snippets shine a light on the important topic of mental illness, I feel like you also need to know some of our back-story to begin to *truly* know my brother or me and how we ended up where we are.

I began recording our back-story in journals years ago. I wrote about my life, my brother, our lives together, our family dynamics, my journey to get help for my other one I know is Jay Neugeboren's, *Imagining Robert*, about his brother's serious bipolar disorder. Jay tells a moving and compassionate story, and Jennifer's is equally as compelling.

I would recommend that anyone with a loved one with mental illness read this book. Indeed, it is really a "must-read."

Finally, I would like to thank Jennifer Ayers-Moore for her bravery in writing this book and her willingness to expose some hard things for the sake of helping others.

Thank you, Jennifer. As we say here at USC: "Fight On!"

Elyn R. Saks, J.D., Ph.D.

Orrin B. Evans Distinguished Professor of Law, Psychology, Psychiatry, and the Behavioral Sciences University of Southern California Gould School of Law

Adjunct Professor of Psychiatry University of California, San Diego, School of Medicine

Director Saks Institute for Mental Health Law, Policy, and Ethics

Faculty New Center for Psychoanalysis

Prelude

One could look at my life and see that it was much like too many others' – a two-time child of divorce; suffered from health issues; a witness to racism; a divorcee; a single, adoptive mother; abandoned and all but forgotten by my absentee father. The way it differs, however, is that my brother – once a promising, double bassist who attended The Juilliard School on scholarship in the 1970s – was diagnosed with schizophrenia and, eventually, ended up homeless on Skid Row in L.A. He was discovered by an L.A. journalist who wrote a book about him that was made into a mainstream, Hollywood movie.

You can read all about this aspect of my brother's life by doing a quick web search. You will even come across interviews with me giving "the real, behind-the-scenes scoop" about my brother and his life. But the things you read or see in the movie about my brother and me are only small snippets of our story. While I am grateful that these snippets shine a light on the important topic of mental illness, I feel like you also need to know some of our back-story to begin to *truly* know my brother or me and how we ended up where we are.

I began recording our back-story in journals years ago. I wrote about my life, my brother, our lives together, our family dynamics, my journey to get help for my brother, our triumphs, my failures, hard lessons learned, and my emotional processing of it all. This book is a compilation of these journal entries, pieced together through multiple entries, over many years. It *is not meant* to be one, cohesive, chronological, tidy work. After all, have you ever met anyone, let alone a caregiver of someone who suffers from a severe mental health condition, to live a simple, tidy, cohesive life? Unlikely.

What this book *is meant* to do is raise awareness for those suffering from mental health conditions, through a first hand account, and stir a desire within all who read it to learn more about mental illness and how it affects a person, their families, friends, caregivers, the mental health community, and our entire society. This has been my all-consuming goal and one of my greatest wishes in life since I was very young – that compassion and help for those with mental health conditions would replace Mental Illness Discrimination and all stigma associated with mental health conditions.

I pray that my brother's and my story stirs that desire within you – to compassionately help people like us end stigma and change the world.

~Jennifer Ayers-Moore

Contents

1. Processional 1
2. Everything Changes 11
3. My Brother Before 27
4. My Mother, My Hero 31
5. Our "Normal" Childhood 41
6. It Isn't Always Easy 53
7. To Treat Or Not To Treat 69
8. My "Iron Sharpens Iron" Marriage 81
9. My Father 89
10. Everything Changes, Again 99
11. Ups And Downs 115
12. A Trip Home 137
13. Losing Our Father 153
14. Where Do We Go From Here 163
15. Hearing Others Music 179
16. Others Like Us 197
17. The Letters 203
18. Recessional 219
19. Appendix A: Blended Chaos 233
20. Appendix B: The Girls 243
21. Works Cited 251
22. Acknowledgements 253

Processional

I noticed something strange happening to me during my junior year at Kent State University. I was having a difficult time concentrating and it went beyond the regular year-end burnout. It felt like a weight throbbing in my head, bearing down in my mind, and painfully threatening to push its way out. I could hear words coming out of people's mouths, but everything seemed foggy. Processing through the fog made it difficult for me to study. I was battling headaches, dizziness, lethargy, excessive thirst, and great weight fluctuations within a two-week period; the burden of it all would often drive me to bed in exhaustion. It felt like I was becoming someone else. It was so very strange. There was something wrong; I thought something was wrong with my brain. I used to say, "I feel like there is a brick in my head." My friends were scared for me. I wanted to fully share with my friends what was going on with me, but I could not bring myself to vocalize what I thought was happening. It became a chore to make them understand my struggle.

I was terrified and wondered if I was developing schizophrenia. Schizophrenia is a chronic and severe psychiatric disorder, as stated by The National Alliance on Mental Illness (www.NAMI.org), which affects how a person thinks, feels, behaves, and can affect the way the person relates to others. It can be debilitating and estimated to affect between 0.25% - 0.65% of adults in the United States. Schizophrenia can also affect a person's mood, called Schizoaffective Disorder. This mental illness had already wreaked havoc in my family before I started showing the weird symptoms that gripped me in terror.

 My older brother, Nathaniel, was diagnosed with schizophrenia when I was a young teen. There was no warning, and it seemed to appear overnight. His diagnosis was a devastating blow to my family. It was scary watching him change as the mental illness began to manifest. At that time, no one knew how to help my brother and the only thing we really knew about schizophrenia was the unpleasant stigma we heard on the streets. Our community and extended family were just as surprised as we were with the diagnosis. Poor education and bewilderment about mental illness during that time led to cruel smirks, hurtful comments, and an overall lack of empathy and alienation for my brother and our immediate family. It was such a scary time for us not knowing how to help Nathaniel nor deal with his increasingly erratic behavior. It was terrifying knowing if symptoms like this could shatter my smart, kind, handsome, talented brother, it could happen to anyone. It could happen to me.

Compass Health Care[1] says the symptoms of schizophrenia are generally divided into three categories:

1. Positive
2. Negative, and
3. Cognitive Symptoms

Positive Symptoms manifest because of the disorder. Positive symptoms include delusions and hallucinations. Negative Symptoms are the absence of behaviors or characteristics because of the disorder. Negative symptoms include emotional flatness or lack of expression; inability to start and follow through with activities; speech, which is brief and devoid of content; and lack of pleasure or interest in life. Cognitive Symptoms affect thought processes because of the disorder. Cognitive symptoms include difficulty prioritizing tasks, difficulty with certain kinds of memory functions, difficulty organizing thoughts, and lack of insight into the difficulties experienced related to the disorder. We never knew nor do we know to this day which symptoms will manifest with my brother.

Nathaniel has shown Positive, Negative and/or Cognitive Symptoms during the darkest days of his illness. I can remember the look of horror and concern on my mother's face when Nathaniel would ramble on about a problem no one could see nor understand, except my brother. I remember asking myself during that challenging

---

[1] (https://www.compasshealthcare.com/consumer-education/)

time in college, "Is that what I sound like trying to explain myself to others?" Did anyone understand me when I tried to explain how I was feeling, or did the words only make sense in my head? I worried if I received those same looks of pity, it could only mean I had met the same fate as my brother – schizophrenia. It had been so unsettling for me to watch mental illness change Nathaniel, I began to allow fear and denial to control me. I felt so scared, I quit talking about what was happening to me, altogether.

    I was diagnosed with Type 1 diabetes at the age of 21. High glucose – not schizophrenia – was the cause of my symptoms. I found myself needing to take daily medication for the first time and was resistant to this change. No one else seemed to be taking my illness seriously, neither did I. I knew my family loved and cared about me, but it felt like my illness took a backseat to Nathaniel's. Nathaniel would tell me diabetes was "a stupid disease." I now know he was just as scared about my diagnosis as I was about his, but his words hurt me. I did not want this new responsibility, so it was not an easy road for me. For too long, I did not take care of myself the way I should have, and my noncompliance with medication made me feel terribly sick those first few years. It took several years of me being sick before I realized I could not help Nathaniel, nor our mom, the way I wished, if I did not first help myself. Once I surrendered and finally got the diabetes under control, I finally felt more like myself again.

For my brother, Nathaniel, his diagnosis of schizophrenia was a different, heart-wrenching story.

    Nathaniel and I were both afflicted with illness in unique ways. Whereas my diagnosis of diabetes had only changed my life, Nathaniel's diagnosis of schizophrenia changed the lives of our entire family. His diagnosis changed my life so drastically I became selfish. I did not know what to do or say to him. I did not know how to share with anyone how I was feeling about all the changes we were going through as a family in the wake of Nathaniel's diagnosis. Unlike me with my diagnosis, Nathaniel started out strong and made a real effort to get better. Unfortunately, his first experience with medication was not a success, because the meds took away his ability to "hear the music."

    You see, my brother was a prodigious musician, so being able to "hear the music" in his mind and deep in his soul was and is everything. Doctors have prescribed many different medications for Nathaniel over the years which were meant to help level out the highs and lows common to schizophrenia, but it has always been a struggle getting him to stick with a treatment which silences the music in his mind. I used to get so angry with him. I would think to myself, "Why wouldn't you want to take medications which are meant to help you feel better?" Once I experienced my own medical crisis though, I realized it was easier said than done. The doctor told me I needed to take medication every single day to feel normal. I was in denial. Surely, he was wrong. I could not fathom the inconvenience and dependency on drugs every day for the rest of my life. I rejected the seriousness of my diagnosis, and occasionally convinced myself I could handle it on my own without medication intervention. My mindset left me feeling sick, helpless, hopeless, and emotionally volatile.

 I am sure others suffering from a mental health condition and their families go through similar things. Having interactions and conversations with a mentally ill loved one who is resistant to the lifestyle changes required to stay healthy can cause a whirlwind of emotions in all who are involved; especially when the one who is sick rejects treatments meant to help them. The idea that Nathaniel is not always going to do what is best for him, like I eventually learned to do, is something I have had to learn to deal with over the years. There is no clear path to healing for any mental illness, including schizophrenia. Families like ours want the same things for our loved ones as every other family – to be well and live happy, productive lives. I have been hoping for that for over 40 years. It may seem silly, but I am still hopeful.

 My brother is doing much better now, but I have learned bad days will never fully go away. One assumes they are accustomed to the daily struggles of a loved one with mental illness until the unexpected comes along, old, or new, and causes a major setback. I am constantly telling people Nathaniel is doing better and he really is in so many ways, but my wishes and hopes do not control his life. My journey with my brother has been such a growing process for us both.

It was hard for me to learn to let go of the need to control and change him, but I have had to because it was impossible for me to keep up with Nathaniel. Still, I hope he has never felt rejected or unloved, because I do love and care for him, so very much. I have also learned other things along our journey. Like, when I say to Nathaniel, "I love you," nine times out of ten he is not going to say it back, and I cannot take it personally. I consider myself blessed if he does reciprocate. I choose to believe he loves me, and occasionally, I will hear a grunt of, "Uh huh, love you."

That is fine with me now, and I will continue to tell him how deeply I love him, whenever I can. I used to have several of my brother's voice mail messages saved and would listen to them from time to time. One message from Nathaniel said, "Jenny you're such a good sister. You're really my best friend." That meant so much to me. He is such a sentimental guy. I always want my brother to understand he is important and holds a great deal of value. I know others feel the same as me. Everything I have done for my brother, both big and small, I have done from the heart. I am not looking for anything nor do I expect anything in return. I just want my brother to know how loved he is.

One of the ways I show my love for my brother is by speaking out for him and others like him since they are not generally able to articulate for themselves. I have gotten to do this through my work for The National Alliance on Mental Illness and the establishment of The Nathaniel Anthony Ayers Foundation, currently in transition to the Friends of Ayers Foundation, which offers informational blogs and podcasts on Facebook and at www.friendsofayers.com. The Foundation was launched after the publication of a book by Steve Lopez about Nathaniel called, *The Soloist: A Lost Dream, an Unlikely Friendship, and the Redemptive Power of Music.* The mission of The Nathaniel Anthony Ayers Foundation was to raise public awareness about mental health and help families who were seeking support for a loved one suffering from mental illness.

    I have come to realize speaking out holds great power; I will continue working toward giving a voice to those who do not know how to speak out. I am learning to be more vocal and open in advocating for my brother and others like him. I have battled with fear of the unknown, stress, worry, embarrassment, sleepless nights, anger, and denial along my journey. I have also hoped and dreamed one day my brother would snap out of it and miraculously be better, like I had hoped with my late husband.

    My husband, Jerry, had been in the hospital for 6 months with kidney failure before he died. I sat by his bedside and experienced the same painful, emotional roller coaster watching him lose his battle as I continue to deal with Nathaniel's battle.

The uniquely different experiences with my husband and my brother have taught me to be open with the battles my family has faced, and my own transparency has made it easier for me to understand Nathaniel's lingering problems. I have dedicated my life to understanding mental illness and hearing my brother's unique music. I did not know what to say before to help him, or others, or myself, but I do now. It is imperative we realize everyone is facing a hidden battle, and the darkness makes victory over those battles seem impossible. Bravely shedding light on our battles may embolden another to speak out, get help, and boldly share the beautiful music of their own lives. I hope my story inspires others dealing with mental illness, their families, and caregivers. Then we can learn and grow together! Knowing Nathaniel is a blessing to me. I wish you could know him, too.

He is such a kind man.
You can see kindness all over his face.
You can see kindness in his eyes.

Everything Changes

"Hear the Music" is a metaphor that means so much more than hearing musical instruments and the sounds they produce. "Hear the Music" is my way of saying to "listen to the music of life," which is something I learned from my brother, Nathaniel. For me, hearing the music means taking the time to really listen to others instead of jumping to conclusions, treating people with respect, and having an open mind about the differences we ALL have. Nathaniel has taught me so much, yet I am still learning who he is and how he hears the music.

My brother, Nathaniel, has always been able to hear the music of life and instruments. Music allowed him to express himself when he had no other voice. I will be the first to admit, I do not always hear the music of life, and I have not always heard my brother's music either. It was hard on me and my family when doctors diagnosed Nathaniel with schizophrenia. It was even harder on my brother though, because mental illness blocked out all music for a while. It made it hard for him to communicate with us and harder for us to understand him. This new season brought many questions with no answers.

Though not everyone is able to express themselves through music like my brother, we all should learn to hear the music of life. We must learn to listen for cues in others indicating they might need our help. We must try to understand others even when it is hard. It has taken me a long time to understand this – to understand Nathaniel – and I am still on the journey to learn from him. His talent, the way he loves, the music he hears. All are as unique as the names he has been known by in different seasons of his life: Nathaniel Anthony Ayers. Tony Ocean. *The Soloist*. My big brother. Sadly, Nathaniel had struggled from the beginning of his diagnosis, because the people he loved the most did not try to hear his music, and if they did, they had difficulty understanding it.

People called my brother "crazy" after his schizophrenia diagnosis. (He was not nor is he crazy; he has a mental health condition.) In the first stages of my brother's illness, it was challenging to separate the brother I used to know from the person he was becoming. I would look at my brother sometimes and feel the same disappointment I felt when we were kids, and he was not paying attention to me. Before the illness manifested, he was just an older brother ignoring his little sister, but everything changed after his diagnosis. Our mom sought treatment for the illness that changed Nathaniel's and our lives forever. He tried a myriad of medications meant to control his highs and lows and to keep him leveled out. But our mother, Floria, understood before anyone else did that this illness meant a change that could ultimately derail his dream of being a successful, classical musician playing in an orchestra.

It was obvious at the time Nathaniel was not ready to let his dream of being a musician die. In the early days of his diagnosis, he was a warrior fighting for his life, genuinely trying to get better. Doctors started him off on a drug called Thorazine and in the following months we saw alarming changes in Nathaniel. He grew lethargic and started gaining weight. We noticed he lost interest in playing music and eventually stopped playing altogether, though we knew he wanted to play. Then he stopped taking his medication.

It was not until much later that Nathaniel told us he could not hear the music while he was on the medication. With medication, he had lost his voice and the only way he had to express himself. When my brother plays, he is speaking to you. If he cannot play, he loses his ability to communicate with the world. Unfortunately, this early experience would shape his feelings toward medication for the rest of his life. Despite changes and improvements in medicine, Nathaniel remained wary of prolonged treatment for an awfully long time because of those first days. He did not want to risk silencing the music again.

Music has taken on the form of medicine for my brother, and I am thankful for my brother's opportunity to study and play music throughout his life since before his diagnosis. He had the opportunity to study music at Harry

E. Davis (where it all started), The Cleveland Music Settlement (where he met Mr. Harry Barnoff), John Hay High School, Ohio University, Juilliard School of Music, The Ohio State University, and The Colorado Music Festival, to name a few. I assumed my brother's taste in music began and ended with classical, but over the years I have learned he loves all music. I had no idea he liked Neil Diamond until he asked his friend, Steve Lopez (author of *The Soloist: A Lost Dream, an Unlikely Friendship, and the Redemptive Power of Music*), to take him to a concert. It was not until we met her at the White House, I discovered Nathaniel loves Patti Labelle, and I later caught him listening to Stevie Wonder. He can find peace and joy in all music.

My brother's education about the music he loves is impressive – the artists, composers, conductors – all of it. It might not be obvious to outsiders, but Nathaniel is an intelligent man. Not only that, Nathaniel is still so talented. During an interview for the television show "60 Minutes," Morley Safer asked Adam Crane, then Los Angeles Philharmonic Orchestra publicist, if Nathaniel was a good musician. He answered, "Either you have it, or you don't. He has it."

Music is such an integral part of Nathaniel's DNA that he thinks I should have studied music like him. He tends to get on me about my lack of music education. He tells me I watch too much TV and enjoy too little music. I did learn to play the drums in high school, but it was never this illness meant a change that could ultimately derail his dream of being a successful, classical musician playing in an orchestra.

It was obvious at the time Nathaniel was not ready to let his dream of being a musician die. In the early days of his diagnosis, he was a warrior fighting for his life, genuinely trying to get better. Doctors started him off on a drug called Thorazine and in the following months we saw alarming changes in Nathaniel. He grew lethargic and started gaining weight. We noticed he lost interest in playing music and eventually stopped playing altogether, though we knew he wanted to play. Then he stopped taking his medication.

It was not until much later that Nathaniel told us he could not hear the music while he was on the medication. With medication, he had lost his voice and the only way he had to express himself. When my brother plays, he is speaking to you. If he cannot play, he loses his ability to communicate with the world. Unfortunately, this early experience would shape his feelings toward medication for the rest of his life. Despite changes and improvements in medicine, Nathaniel remained wary of prolonged treatment for an awfully long time because of those first days. He did not want to risk silencing the music again.

Music has taken on the form of medicine for my brother, and I am thankful for my brother's opportunity to study and play music throughout his life since before his diagnosis. He had the opportunity to study music at Harry

E. Davis (where it all started), The Cleveland Music Settlement (where he met Mr. Harry Barnoff), John Hay High School, Ohio University, Juilliard School of Music, The Ohio State University, and The Colorado Music Festival, to name a few. I assumed my brother's taste in music began and ended with classical, but over the years I have learned he loves all music. I had no idea he liked Neil Diamond until he asked his friend, Steve Lopez (author of *The Soloist: A Lost Dream, an Unlikely Friendship, and the Redemptive Power of Music*), to take him to a concert. It was not until we met her at the White House, I discovered Nathaniel loves Patti Labelle, and I later caught him listening to Stevie Wonder. He can find peace and joy in all music.

My brother's education about the music he loves is impressive – the artists, composers, conductors – all of it. It might not be obvious to outsiders, but Nathaniel is an intelligent man. Not only that, Nathaniel is still so talented. During an interview for the television show "60 Minutes," Morley Safer asked Adam Crane, then Los Angeles Philharmonic Orchestra publicist, if Nathaniel was a good musician. He answered, "Either you have it, or you don't. He has it."

Music is such an integral part of Nathaniel's DNA that he thinks I should have studied music like him. He tends to get on me about my lack of music education. He tells me I watch too much TV and enjoy too little music. I did learn to play the drums in high school, but it was never my whole life like it is for Nathaniel. He still remembers the first rat-a-tat-tat I learned to play during my marching band days, and I still play on a drum set in my basement sometimes. Nathaniel hears the music and loves instruments so much; he chose to stay in the basement with my drum set and the instruments he brought with him when he visited me in August of 2010. He simply hears things in a way the rest of us do not. He may not hear it the same way he did when he was younger, but he is still in tune with all the music he hears in the world. Nathaniel truly hears the music – instrumental and the music of life. In speaking with my brother, you find a knowledgeable and witty conversationalist with whom it is great to discuss instrumental music and the music he sees flowing from life.

You may not be an instrumentalist, like my brother, but you can hear and make music, nonetheless. The "music" you hear may be gardening, walking, reading, writing, sports, or by doing something which gives you a real sense of peace and freedom. But we must respect others for the unique music they hear. Peace and freedom for you might mean chaos and no freedom for another. If no harm comes from it, we must allow everyone to march to the beat of their own drum, hearing their own music, and creating their own concerts. Sure, it can be hard to not automatically judge one another for their unique music, but I know we desperately need each of us to change our minds toward this type of judgment considering how strangers have treated my brother. We must allow others to hear and create music that is beautiful to them.

    The music I hear is in advocating for others. I find peace in helping others to achieve their own kind of peace. The music I hear is my desire to see Nathaniel, and others like him, happy and thriving in their lives and for their families to receive the aid they need to advocate for their family members. I know from my own personal experience, when a family member is suffering there is a trickle-down effect on everyone else in the family. I want to make sure there are programs helping all those affected by mental illness. The only way we can end the stigma associated with mental illness is to start a conversation and encourage others to speak out. Changing individual attitudes toward those with mental illness is paramount to the lives of people like my brother. I "hear the music" as I work toward fulfilling our mother's dream of helping her son, others like him, and their families.

    Mom realized she was going to have to help Nathaniel indirectly, as he was sometimes resistant to help. It was hard to see my brother rejecting my mother's efforts, but I know his own mind was tormenting him. She also realized other individuals and families were going through the same troubles we were experiencing. So, she decided to reach out, speak out, and help in every way she could. She wanted to treat others the same way she hoped they would treat her son. She would often tell me, "Jesus was turned away by his own people and he didn't give up, so we can't give up." Through it all, Mom never gave up the good fight; she never gave up on her son despite the fact it was hard for her to clearly hear the music in her own life.

Mom was going through a lot when she began advocating. She was struggling with difficulties in her marriage and her own son lashing out at her in what seemed, to her, like deliberate vengeance. She used to tell me that it was not really Nathaniel at those moments; the illness invoked frustration, which could be misinterpreted as anger and made him someone else. Despite sometimes feeling helpless to help her own son, she busied herself orchestrating a concert with the unique music she heard all around her. She decided to invite ladies into our home who were struggling with mental illness and lack of support in their own lives and cook meals for them. Mom believed very much in the power of paying it forward. She made sure that others felt the love, care, and support she wished for her own family.

This was hard on Mom, but it helped her take some of the focus off my brother and allowed her to help someone when Nathaniel refused help. She began reaching out to every resource she knew of while she helped others who were experiencing mental illness. She was proactive in seeking help, never sat around waiting for change, and was never ashamed to ask for prayer. At the time, I did not have much hope for the work, but Mom always believed we were making a difference and said she could not do it without me. Our mother was a powerhouse in finding help for my brother. She often asked me to help write letters and proposals to our local government, looking for help that was already available and advocating for help where there seemed to be none.

Our letters did get the attention of at least one official. Virgil Brown, Chairman of the Cleveland Board of Commissioners, often called mom to offer suggestions. He led Mom to The Murtis Taylor Health Services System, a countywide center that did outreach programs in Behavioral Health, Addiction, Youth, Family and Senior services. I went to the center with her on several occasions. Eventually, Mom heard from the mayor of Cleveland, Carl Stokes, but it was really Virgil who helped our family the most. Virgil stayed connected with our family for years and even helped get my first summer job that later led to my first full-time job after college. Meanwhile, Mom continued to press on listening to the music of those she could help.

Eventually, Mom "heard the music" of a lady with a mental illness, by the name of Thomasina Powell, whom she met on a venture once to rescue Nathaniel. Mom used to pick up Ms. Powell and bring her to our house to visit, since her own family did not see her often, or at all. The visits became more frequent, and before I knew it, Ms. Powell was living with us full-time. I was angry with this new development, at first. How could we help this stranger when we could not seem to help Nathaniel? Did he not deserve to have our full attention? I finally worked up the nerve to ask Mom why we were helping this woman when we already had Nathaniel who needed our help. She told me, "I am doing for Ms. Powell what I would like for someone to do for Tony." (Tony was Mom's nickname for Nathaniel.) Her answer shut me down and from then on, I learned to deal with Ms. Powell's presence. I did not realize then how right my mother was; I was not always going to be able to help my brother, but someone else might enter his life and help him the way Mom helped others. This was an important lesson I hold close to my heart to this day.

Ms. Powell was instrumental in teaching Mom and me how to approach Nathaniel. She often had conversations with voices only she could hear. It was alarming to see and hear, at first, and neither of us quite knew how to deal with these uninvited, invisible guests. Mom tried different things to calm Ms. Powell down when the voices made an appearance, but nothing worked until one day when Ms. Powell started arguing with her invisible friends. I was in my room, but I overheard Mom ask her, "Are you tired of fussing with those voices, because I am certainly tired of hearing the arguments!" Then Ms. Powell and Mom joined each other in laughter.

The conversations were less frequent after that day, and after months of loud and often alarming arguments, I was able to laugh as well. Something about the way my mother reacted that day helped Ms. Powell move past those voices. It gave Mom hope that we could help Nathaniel with his own issues one day. That pivotal moment provided Mom with the motivation to keep looking for answers. I overheard Mom telling her sister, Aunt Ollie, about that victory on the phone.

Prior to that breakthrough, I remember my brother had a troublesome time with Ms. Powell being in our home. He acted like he hated her. His attitude did not seem to affect her however, and she was never afraid of him. Ms. Powell stood her ground with Nathaniel. She was faithful about taking her medicine, stayed clean and kept her room tidy. She even helped with other household chores from time to time. She enjoyed being around a family and having people to support her, especially my mom.

Mom would do Ms. Powell's hair and give her nice outfits to wear. Ms. Powell was a tall, slender lady and Mom used to say, "she could have been a model." You could not tell Ms. Powell that she was not a supermodel; she was an astute, proud woman whose only issue was her mental health. Sometimes, Mom and Ms. Powell would leave our house to visit family, but they would also just sit around the house, all decked out, even if they were not going anywhere. I believe Mom did that for Ms. Powell. Mom used to say that Ms. Powell was a "Diamond in the Rough." Ms. Powell thoroughly enjoyed hearing Nathaniel play classical music, hanging on every note he played with bated breath, and to our surprise, we learned she also played the piano.

Mom said she heard someone playing the piano one day, and upon investigating, discovered Ms. Powell trying to find her way around the keyboard. It did not take long for her to rediscover her skill and love for music. Ms. Powell began playing every day and even started singing along. Her love of music earned her a great deal of respect from my brother. You could easily see Ms. Powell was a respectful and proud woman, and it was clear Ms. Powell was making as much of an impact in Mom's life as Mom was making in Ms. Powell's.

    I did not see the gravity of what Mom was doing at that time, but I certainly saw it years later. I smile when I think about how my brother would shake his head, get very agitated or just walk away when he would hear Ms. Powell having a conversation with the voices she heard. I even remember when he realized that she was not talking as much anymore. He listened from outside her door, made a "Hmm" sound, smirked, and walked away.

    Mom insisted Ms. Powell take her medicine downstairs at the kitchen table as part of her daily routine. One reason was to make sure she did take them, and I am sure the second was to be an inspiration to Nathaniel. It was beautiful to watch the way Mom generously and overtly helped others to hear their own music that she hoped, I suspect, would model the way for Nathaniel.

    Ms. Powell became physically ill after about two years with us and became hospitalized while I was away at college. I sent cards to her while she was in the hospital, but by then, I truly only communicated with her through Mom. She ended up dying of cancer. I vaguely remember only one visit to her, ever, from one of her family members. That weighed on Mom, and she did not want Ms. Powell to feel alone like she hoped Nathaniel would never feel alone. Mom did not have it in her heart to abandon Ms. Powell, and she never did.

I am thankful Ms. Powell was a part of my life for a brief time. She was a nice lady. We had become her surrogate family. Despite the lack of presence from her biological family, I DO NOT have any negative judgment toward them - NONE. My wish, however, is that Ms. Powell's family could have had the chance to see how she had grown and how she had gained a sense of "normalcy." She stopped combatively talking to the voices and looked well. She had us to depend on and was happy, even though I am sure she missed her biological family. I imagine the separation was hard on her family, too. She was such an intelligent and uniquely talented person. Mom and Ms. Powell's beautiful, symbiotic relationship help them, both, to grow and become healthier versions of themselves.

My brother also began to grow and become a healthier person when a man named Steve Lopez heard Nathaniel's music – literally and metaphorically. Steve recognized Nathaniel needed help and treated him like Mom treated Ms. Powell. "I am doing for Ms. Powell what I want someone to do for Tony" – Mom's wish had come to pass. She was often successful in finding help for Nathaniel, but nothing compared to the opportunities that came from the book Steve wrote called *The Soloist: A Lost*

Dream, an Unlikely Friendship, and the Redemptive Power of Music. The book, and subsequent movie, created big opportunities for Nathaniel, although he never cared much for them. I will admit, I was leery of the whole book and movie deal at first, but I will be forever grateful to Steve Lopez for taking an interest in my brother.

Nathaniel found a new friend in Steve who went out of his way to help my brother. Steve helped create opportunities for Nathaniel to play music, travel and was in his element. There were challenges, however, and anytime traveling came up, we never knew if Nathaniel would make the trip. He constantly changed his mind about traveling until the day of the trip, even when everything was booked and ready to go. It is still like that to this day, albeit better.

During that overwhelming time with the book and movie, I saw a lot of kindness and a lot of deception. Many individuals we were meeting said things like, "We're a family now." I wanted to believe that was true since I had seen Nathaniel ostracized for so much of his life. Everything that was happening gave him a chance at a better life, and that whole experience certainly gave him the time of his life. He felt respected which is not a feeling he knows well anymore, sadly. People who would never have spoken to him before stopped to say "hello" and ask for autographs and pictures.

In hindsight, I know I could have overseen Nathaniel's business affairs a little better during that time, but I was not familiar with Hollywood. In the moment, I could only see people trying to help my brother, so I settled and took what they gave him. Everyone had an opinion on the running of Nathaniel's business at that time, too – not always positive opinions either; regardless, I never let what happened nor anyone's opinions of the experience change my respect and appreciation of Steve and all those who were genuinely trying to help my brother.

    As the dust settles from the Hollywood frenzy, I can see Nathaniel is missing the attention and respect he garnered during that time, most of all. He does still get an occasional invitation to play and Steve still tries to help Nathaniel honor those invitations. I do not expect everyone to make the kind of sacrifices Steve has. He will be the first to admit that like most journalists, the story was his primary motivation in the beginning. It is not every day a journalist gets to write about meeting a man who attended Juilliard and lives homeless on the streets of LA. It is also not every day the journalist becomes friends with that homeless man. The story turned out to be much more than a story, and it changed both their lives for the better; it changed my life, as well.

    Steve did not set out to become Nathaniel's friend and ally, but that is exactly what happened. He gave of himself to Nathaniel while writing articles about him. Their budding friendship and those articles opened the floodgates of concern from the public paving the way to make a difference for all who have a mental health condition. Unfortunately, not every person in need of help is going to find a Steve Lopez. Can you imagine how much better the lives of the mentally ill would be if they could find help from someone like Steve Lopez or my mom? Making life better for those who suffer from a mental health condition would make life better for us all.

"The only way we can end the stigma associated with mental illness is to start a conversation and encourage others to speak out."

My Brother Before

When I was a child, my family and I went through a particularly tough time. We were distraught when my biological father chose to start a new life in another state. I felt displaced and out of control from losing my father and started having what I would describe as "out of body experiences." I felt like I was looking down at my own body watching what was happening from the outside. It was like I was frozen, yet I was functioning. I could see my body on the ground going through the motions, but it felt like I was somewhere else and not really experiencing it. To his credit, Nathaniel really took care of me then.

My brother was always looking out for me and spent as much time as he could with me. I was always close to him because he really took care of me then. Our sister, Del, was always noticeably quiet when we were kids, so I never felt like I could talk to her back then (though time has helped our communication.) So, it always felt like it was Nathaniel and me against the world when we were kids. He is no longer the same person he was back then, otherwise I am sure he would still be trying to take care of me. I miss having the brother I once knew. I keep many fond memories of my brother from my childhood.

I will never forget one of my favorite memories of Nathaniel and me was the day he asked me to play football with him and his friends when we still lived on East 95th street. He was always into sports when we were young. He loved playing football and baseball. He and his friends played football in the street even though we had a, seemingly, huge backyard. I always enjoyed watching my big brother play sports with his friends. I looked up to him. I know God gave me that love. I was totally surprised when Nathaniel called me into the football game with his friends that day. I felt such a sense of happiness and pride that he gave me the chance to take part.

 I lined up for the snap not knowing what I was doing, and he threw the football to me. I caught it and he said, "Run!" I ran as fast as I could, and I got a touchdown! NO ONE even tried to touch or tackle me. I did not find out until much later my brother had forbidden anyone to touch me. This memory of Nathaniel including and protecting me warms my heart. It reminds me of how much he has always loved and wanted to protect me - his little sister. And since his diagnosis, I have wanted to do the same for him. The playtime I spent with Nathaniel helped me feel protected, brave, and sometimes, invincible.

 I remember trying to keep up with my brother and his friends one day as they played hide and seek. They were running quickly, and I unsuccessfully tried to match their speed. They ran up then back down the steps of an apartment building that was on the corner, across from Mom's beauty shop. I had run to the second floor trying to catch up to the boys when I noticed Nathaniel was in the wonderful cook, and her signature dessert dish was peach cobbler. Family would always ask Mom to bring her cobbler to our family outings, especially during the holidays. Our mother's siblings (Ollie, Martha, Bernice, Elmo, Jesse, James & Ralph) were a lot like her. Everything she and her sisters (including my uncle's wives) cooked was fabulous. We had great fun in my youth with our close-knit, extended family which also included my aunts, Mattie, Willa & Louise. I remember spending every holiday together until Nathaniel got sick. It seemed to me that our holiday gathering invitations changed after Nathaniel got sick, because no one knew how to deal with the situation of his mental health and the effect it had on our family.

    Our mom had been career-oriented, goal driven, gorgeous, and determined to achieve her goals. As a little girl, I simply adored my mother. Nathaniel revered Mom and thought that she was the most special person on the face of the earth; it was a special mother-son bond. We really loved our parents. Nathaniel was especially proud of Mom's business savvy and her drive to be successful with her business. That was one of her traits everyone seemed to notice. Mom loved to do hair and she was great at it.

    Mom had many loyal customers at Flo's Beauty Lounge, including my aunts and cousins who consistently went to mom for hair care for years. Most of the female relatives in our big family went to Mom to get their hair done. Mom was the inspiration for some of my cousins

My Mother, My Hero

I vividly remember living at the dead-end of East 95th Street in Cleveland, Ohio. Mom's very own hairdressing business, Flo's Beauty Lounge, sat at the corner of East 95th Street and St. Claire, just down the street from our house and across from the apartment building from which I naively took flight, only to hit the ground like a lead ball. I remember she would drive the correct direction on the one-way street to get to work then back up the same street going the wrong direction to come home. It was wrong, but it was creative. I laugh when I think about how she would just whip the car in the yard from the wrong direction. Nathaniel, Del and I would go down to Mom's beauty shop after school to do our homework and help with chores if Mom had not yet made it home. There was always music playing at Flo's and typically was not anything very bouncy or upbeat. It was always something like smooth jazz or a soft voice singing a song. I sometimes wonder if it was listening to the music playing in our mother's shop that sparked the musical fire in my brother's heart. Our mom was amazing, and she was a "jack of all trades."

Mom was able to fix nearly anything, or tried to at least, before getting someone else to do the job. She was a moments, our family seemed fine – so did my brother. When I remember our good and tough times, I find myself wondering what happened to my brother.

Questions I asked myself for a long time:

- What was the pivotal moment that changed Nathaniel? Our life seemed fine to me despite what happened between our parents.
- Did something in our youth cause him to develop a mental health condition?
- Could we have stopped his mental health condition from developing?
- Should we have done something differently?
- What could we have done to change the course of his life and to make him stronger?

I came to realize there is nothing we could have done. It was Nathaniel's destiny to be who he is today. As a witness to many things my brother has been through, I will say, with certainty, he is the most courageous man I have ever known. And the most courageous woman I have ever known? Our mother, Floria.

lead and back on the ground. I wanted to catch up, so I jumped from the balcony and hit the ground concrete like a lead ball.

    I remember how it felt falling from the sky for what seemed like an eternity but lasted only a second. Nathaniel came back to make sure that I was okay, giving up his lead in the hide and seek game - always my protector. The fall did not hurt me, thank God. Shaken up, I decided to go home rather than play more games with him and his friends. Though my jump ended my game that day, I cherish the fond memories of playing with Nathaniel and feeling his protection of me.

    Despite the tremendous amount of pain and loss my siblings and I lived through as children, we did have some good times at home. Our family tradition was to sit down to family dinners after we finished our chores at the end of the day. Our mother diligently kept everything in its place and taught us to do the same. The house was always spotless and smelled fresh. I remember when we got new furniture and our first color TV. We had to stick a plastic film on the TV screen to see color back then. We were so fascinated by the 3 colors on that film – red, yellow, and green – that we watched TV together for hours that first evening. TV has advanced and spoiled me, these days, to the point where I do not think I could sit and watch those old shows anymore. At the time, though, it was a special reward for completing our chores. Marveling at that TV allowed us to do something fun as a family, and in those learning to do hair. Mom's appointment book was always full, and she served most of her customers for a long time. Her specialty was hair care and growth. She was an excellent stylist who could cut styles to perfection even though she always tried to avoid cutting hair short since she loved long hair.

Mom took excellent care of our hair, and she kept us well-groomed from head to toe. She was one of the first hair stylists to do hair weaving in the area and trained other stylists to weave. I even learned to barber from mom which helped me earn extra change while in college.

Mom loved for her shop to be beautiful, clean, and comfortable for all her customers. She was great at using creative décor to make her shop look as classy as possible. She even helped style models for local fashion shows. I remember Mom had an obligation to do hair for a fashion show one Saturday night. Our father did not want her to go, so an argument ensued. "You're not going," he said. "I have to go. They're expecting me, and I'm the only beautician scheduled," Mom insisted. She was dedicated to her clients and her craft.

Mom looked gorgeous after she dressed to go out. She would always wear a beautiful dress, nice high heel shoes and carried a jazzy clutch bag. I think the bag is what would sometimes make my father snap in a fit of jealousy. I remember Mom went to make a call on our old rotary phone before she left for a fashion show one evening. Our father snatched it out of her hand and busted it on the floor. I never really saw them argue before that. That was the first time I had ever seen my father belligerent and angry enough to break something, including my heart. I never understood why he begrudged my mom her success with Flo's and with the fashion shows. After that, the air grew thick in our home as tension developed between my parents.

I could sense something was different, but at five years old, I was too young to understand the problems my parents were having in their marriage. My parents separated, divorced and we ended up moving out of our home when I was seven years old. As I got older, I started to understand what the problem had been. Although I did not initially know to label it as such, I eventually realized my father was extremely insecure about my mother's desire to be a hardworking, successful businesswoman.

As a little girl, I always wanted to hang out with my father. Our family went to church together every Sunday for Sunday school and regular church service then to bible study on Wednesdays. My place in the car was next to my father in the front seat. I never had to sit in the backseat like Nathaniel and Del. One Sunday we took a detour to church. My father told me I needed to get in the back seat so his friend, Miss Gotel, could sit up front. Five-year-old me could not understand why I had to give up my seat for Miss Gotel. Why did I have to sit in the backseat? Why could she not sit in the backseat? Who is this person? I remember the confusion on my siblings' faces as well.

In this photo, Mom was a model in a fashion show. She was also the hair stylist for the show.

My brother said something to me as I moved to the back seat, and I quietly mumbled under my breath, "Why do I have to sit in the back?" I got in trouble for the mumble. My father had mistaken it for a curse word, although he never asked me what I had actually said. It made my morning even more miserable. Ms. Gotel came out and took her place – my place – in the front seat. She seemed in quite a good mood even though the three of us kids were not. Something was so wrong with that scenario.

We finally made it to the church where we went to our own Sunday School classes then on together to the church service, but my broken heart was still aching. I was not happy, nor did I hear much of the lesson that day. Everyone noticed. After church we took Miss Gotel home and then we went home. As we pulled into the driveway, I ran into the house to tell my mother about my terrible morning.

I practically leapt from the moving car to bolt in the house saying, "I had to sit in the backseat, so Miss Gotel could ride up front." Mom looked up in shock at our father. He could not look her in the eyes. He dropped his head, and I knew then it was not about me sitting in the backseat. I was not sure what was going on and I was not sure if my siblings did either. After that episode, the atmosphere in our home changed into one not friendly at all; it was like a storm cloud had set up shop in our house.

Our parents were not speaking much anymore. I did not understand it at the time, but looking back, I can see my father was never secure in his relationship with my smart, determined, and strong mother. Then things seemed to really go downhill in our household.

Mom worked long hours and usually rested on Sunday. One Sunday morning, Mom decided to go to church. She became furious when she could not find her watch. I was the only one home with her at the time, because my siblings had left with our father. Mom was moving about in an unusual way, still she took the time to make sure I was nicely dressed in a nice skirt and blouse, combed my hair, and put on my coat with an aggression which made me feel uncomfortable.

We rushed to the church which was not far. One of the deacons, Brother Ivy, tried to cut us off as we approached the door. Mr. Ivy and his wonderful family were like our family; they loved us, and we loved them. Mom said to him, "Get out of my way, Brother Ivy." Brother Ivy uncomfortably stepped aside for us and did not try to follow. I am guessing he knew what was happening even though I did not.

My mother practically dragged me down the steps and over to the candy stand Miss Gotel was working. Mom told Miss Gotel she wanted her watch back. Ms. Gotel replied as she looked at her wrist, "this was a gift." Mom informed Miss Gotel she had received that watch as a gift from my father first. I could see Ms. Gotel was getting nervous. Mom had a very stern look on her face as she looked directly into Miss Gotel's eyes. I remember thinking

37

how good all that candy looked, but I dared not ask for any at that moment. The watch was exactly something Mom would have liked; it was beautiful and elegant with diamonds and gold band – very sleek and feminine.

Mom repeated, "Give me my watch!" Miss Gotel was not moving fast enough, so Mom grabbed her arm and snatched it off. She told Miss Gotel to never touch her jewelry again.

Mom was quiet on the ride home, which made the short trip seem twice as long. I could see how hurt and upset she was, but at that time, I did not know if it was about my father or the watch, not realizing they were one in the same. My father and siblings were already home when we got there. They had no idea what had just happened when Mom told my father never to take her things out of the house again. Our father did not say a thing, but he looked embarrassed. I still remember the look on my siblings' faces. I never told anyone what I was feeling. I felt like they should have known, since I noticed everyone else was behaving differently – more distant.

Nathaniel stopped playing with his friends as often and Del never seemed to be close to anyone. Mom still worked hard, still drove the correct way down the street to work then reversed the wrong way to come home. She cooked, cleaned, and took care of us, but she was not talking very much – neither did my brother nor sister. We were a quiet family anyway, but the silence between us was deafening after that. I remember looking at my brother wishing he could read my mind and I could know what he was thinking.

I had wanted him to know how sad and lonely I was. Now, I wonder if all the silence had anything to do with how his life turned out. Did Nathaniel develop schizophrenia because of lack of or improper communication? I wonder if things would have turned out differently for him had our family gotten help back then. Would he have still become *The Soloist*? Would mental illness have affected our family?

My father moved out not long after the episode with Mom's watch, but he still came around to take us to church and do things around the house. That totally confused me. Why was he messing with things around the house if he did not live there and was still talking to Ms. Gotel? The thing between him and Miss Gotel was common knowledge at church, yet she continued to work the candy stand. I never went near it again, because even though I was incredibly young, I knew something would not have been right about visiting the stand where she was working. I still wanted that candy, but I stayed away to avoid my thoughts which wondered from where or whom her jewelry had come. She would not look me directly in the face, but I could feel her taunting eyes on me. I do not know how she treated my siblings.

When I thought more about what had happened, I realized mom must have known before then something was going on between my father and Miss Gotel. I was just a child, but the chill, the tension, and the changes between my parents were obvious — even to me. I was so grateful to have gotten through that time in our lives. I felt uncertainty and sadness when we moved away from that community, but I was not at all sad about leaving that church; after all, it was a terribly painful moment for a little girl. To this day, neither my brother nor sister have said a word to me about Miss Gotel and that ride to church. Whenever I try to talk with my siblings about our past with our father, Nathaniel changes the subject, and my sister says she does not remember much about it.

Our "Normal" Childhood

My mom, Aunt Ollie, Del, Nathaniel, and I watched my father fly off to California when I was seven years old. Ms. Gotel had already moved there. I remember feeling oddly upbeat trying to exist in the middle of what I will call "the fog." We were going to the Cleveland Hopkins airport. That meant adventure, right? What could be so bad about that? I had never been to the airport before and it was exciting for me. I was still too young to really appreciate what was happening. I did not understand this trip meant long term separation from my father for our family. I realize in hindsight my brother and sister had done the math long before our father left and did not share the sum with me. I think they may have thought I was just a kid and could not have grasped what his leaving meant anyway.

We watched our father get on the jet and look out the window at us. We kept waving and he waved back. I could still see him looking at us as the jet backed up on the runway, but he stopped waving. That stung a little, but I was ready when mom said, "Ok let's go." Nathaniel and Del were quiet as usual. I can still remember what Nathaniel wore as he strode ahead of us to walk by himself; he was always a snappy dresser and was well groomed. I starkly remember Nathaniel's attire on this occasion, because his behavior was more distant. This day, he wore dressy gray slacks and a gray and black sweater which zipped up the front. Del was also a classy dresser; she was always coordinated and clean. We were all nicely dressed to watch our father board that airplane to start his new life, not knowing how it would play out.

 I ran to catch up with my brother. I tried to hold his hand, but he was not interested. He only gave me a half smile; I could feel his pain. It was clear in his and everyone else's face. I was only seven years old and felt utterly alone. Our father had left for a place called California on a huge jet and no one was talking – not even Mom. There were hundreds of people around me, yet no one could, nor would, connect with my loss.

 What had just happened? I could tell my brother and sister were feeling something too, but they did not share with me and I was too young to discern what they were feeling. Our father left us long before he got on the plane that day, but it still felt fresh.

 Aunt Ollie told me a story about Mom after my parent's divorce; a story I did not fully understand until my thirties and I doubt my siblings ever did. After the divorce, my siblings and I were at Aunt Ollie's one day waiting for Mom to pick us up. She did not show. I later found out Mom had checked herself into the hospital because she felt like she was on the verge of a nervous breakdown after the divorce and with everything she had gone through with our father. Aunt Ollie said she was concerned the state might take us with our father gone and Mom in the hospital. So, she said she marched down to the hospital and told Mom, "You have a business to run and a family to take care of; there is no time for this!"

Aunt Ollie said though she knew it was hard on Mom, she left the hospital and never looked back. Aunt Ollie told me she knew Mom made it through because she could not stand the thought of failing. Mom and I never spoke of it. Odd things began to happen in our lives after my father left and in the wake of Mom working to take her life back.

I remember coming home from school one day to what seemed like 100 kids on my front porch. My sister, Del, had locked herself in the house because a girl wanted to fight her. I later learned the girl was jealous of how nicely Del dressed for school. I do not know how it resolved, but the kids never came back. I assume that situation was frightening for Del even though she never told me how she felt about it. I recently asked her about it, and she did not even remember the incident.

Nathaniel, on the other hand, did not have anything that exciting happen for the final year we remained on East 95th street. He did start spending time with his friends again, but not as much as he once had. He chose to spend a little more time at Flo's Beauty Lounge instead, and he occasionally found time to do things with me.

Two gentlemen were also taking an interest in my mother, during that peculiar and changing time in our lives. Those men visited regularly then after some time, only one was coming around. His name was Alexander Mangrum. When I was eight years old and what seemed out of the blue, Mom told us to pack our things because we were moving. Again, my quiet siblings and I did not ask a single question. We just packed up our house, loaded the boxes in a big truck, hopped in our car and drove to a house on Churchill Avenue.

Alexander Mangrum introduced us to his children for the first time when we arrived at our new home on Churchill; well, it was the house we moved to, but it never felt much like home. He had four children and none of them seemed the least bit happy about our arrival. I wanted to run somewhere – anywhere – to hide. The two Mangrum girls in the family thought my brother was cute and were nice to him right off the bat. The two Mangrum boys were guarded and did not seem to like anybody. The seven of us kids just stood there in shock trying to figure out what was happening; or maybe it was just me who was bewildered, since I was so young.

Mom uprooted us Ayers children from OUR house on East 95th Street and merged with the four Mangrum children in THEIR house on Churchill Avenue. None of us kids got the chance to get to know each other before we became a blended family. The Mangrum children made it clear we Ayers children were on their turf, and that made for an extremely turbulent transition. I wonder how any of us made it out in one piece. The things that happened in our early years as the blended Mangrum family were completely deranged (see "APPENDIX A" for a collection of Ayers/Mangrum stories.) Nathaniel was developing the mental illness, yet he did not try to bring physical harm to our stepsiblings the way they did to us; he always tried to fit in.

I do not want to sound like I am bashing the Mangrum family because I am not. I came to realize the Mangrum children were hurting and bitter, because they did not get the opportunity to grieve the loss of their mother who had died not long before we arrived. It does not excuse some of the terrible things they did to us Ayers kids but realizing where those kids were coming from helped me to forgive and put the hurt behind me, eventually. It took a long time for our relationships in the Mangrum house to improve, and as I struggled to grasp everything, which was happening at that time, the question, "Why?" always plagued me. I found helpful solace listening to music.

The song "500 Miles" by Peter, Paul, and Mary was popular during that time in my life. I repeatedly played that song and sang it at the top of my lungs. I felt so much freedom wailing that song even though the words made me sad. Mom would call me to the top of the landing – my stage – every time we had company, so I could sing that song for them. She had no clue how the song made me feel. No one knew how that song broke me down. Mom was just proud I could sing it so well. I never told her of the painful emotions it stirred in me. I knew Nathaniel and Del understood even though I never verbalized my feelings to them. I just knew, deep down, my siblings felt the same emotions the song stirred in me.

I annoyed everyone in the house on Churchill, because I played that album so much. There were four songs, especially, which made me think of our father leaving us: "500 Miles," "If I Had a Hammer," "This Land Is Your Land," and "Leaving on a Jet Plane." I would string the lyrics of the songs together in a mashup, trying to make sense of what I was feeling: "Surely they missed the train…and if they had a hammer, they would hammer out love between brothers and sisters…and if they had a song, they would sing it all over this land…and maybe our father would hear it…because this land was their land too, from California to the New York Island." California for crying out loud! "Leaving on a Jet Plane" cut especially deep as it painfully reminded me of seeing my father with his packed bags that day at the airport where he said goodbye and left us behind as he flew away.

Hearing that song made me wonder if that was how my mom felt? I did not know, but I chose to feel it for her. I kept thinking, "Maybe Peter, Paul and Mary know us." I never knew if those songs affected Nathaniel and Del like they did me. They dug into the core of my soul and chipped away at my heart. I would listen to them, cry and hide, then wipe away my tears if I heard someone coming. The ironic thing is my mother gave that album to me. She bought it because she heard me singing "500 Miles." Getting that album prompted me to save all my chore money so I could buy more albums.

That Peter, Paul and Mary album still stands out from among the collection I built, because it helped me navigate my loss of self-confidence when we moved to Churchill Avenue and became a blended family with the Mangrum's. No matter how difficult the transition was between us and the Mangrum children, I have some fond memories of my stepfather, Alexander, including his care for my sister, Landria, born to him and my mother.

Alexander would bounce Landria singing, "Jack go around the sunshine. Jack go around the moon. Jack go around the sunshine every afternoon, noon, noon, noon!" She would laugh and laugh. That song would lift Landria's entire mood even if she were crying or sad. Alexander also tried to communicate with Nathaniel, and once Nathaniel really started excelling in music, Alexander insisted our stepbrother, Michael, learn to play the cello; I suspected he did not want Nathaniel to outshine Michael.

Michael played the cello, even though he really did not want to. By this time, we were doing a little better as a blended family, and that experience made Michael appreciate Nathaniel more. Whenever he got a chance, he would ask for Nathaniel's help, which Nathaniel appreciated.

Michael died at school from a heart attack on October 17, 1969. He was 15 years old. Apparently, Michael had a heart condition, even though our parents never told us about it. His death broke all our hearts. I can only imagine what it did to my brother. To this day, I remember what a motivated and likable person my stepfather, Alexander Mangrum, was despite the challenges we faced blending two families.

Alexander was outgoing, social and he liked to dress well, much like Nathaniel. He was a popular electrical contractor and people wondered how he got so many contracts for work with the city. He made it a point to be at the right place at the right time; more than that, he was easy to like.

Alexander was also a big tipper. I do not think I will ever forget how he would say, "When you go out to eat and your waiter is good to you, be good to her or him. So, the next time you come back you won't have anything to worry about." You should have seen how servers would almost fight to wait on his table. I tip well, too, and I know that came from him. Alexander would also say, "the early bird catches the worm" and "put some pep in your step!" He would exclaim, "there you go" when I did walk peppy.

Alexander Mangrum died in 2012. I am grateful for the valuable things I learned from him despite the challenges our blended family endured. And through all these challenges, our biological father was never a source of support for me, nor my siblings.

Even though I wish our father had been there for me, I wish even more that he would have been there for my brother. Nathaniel never directly shared this with me, but I know he kept reaching out to our biological father who rejected him time, and time again. Through the abandonment of our father and the challenges of learning to blend with the Mangrum's, Nathaniel continued to be a loving, thoughtful, big brother to me, pushing through his own pain, and bringing moments of joy to my life. I vividly remember the day Nathaniel bought kites for us to fly at the school playground.

That day we flew kites was such an awesome day! I remember thinking he dressed improperly for the playground, since he wore dressy clothes and a fedora. I did not want to ruin the moment though, so I said nothing. We noticed a few other people flying kites when we reached the playground. I was so excited to be hanging out with Nathaniel and at the thought of flying a kite.

A girl who liked my brother came over to say hello as we began to set up the kites. (Girls have seemed to always gravitate to Nathaniel. You can read more about this in APPENDIX B: THE GIRLS.) Nathaniel said, "Hello," then turned back to me to show me how to fly the kite. He said, "Watch me, so you can do the same thing." The wind was blowing, and I willed his kite to fly as high as the others. As the kite started reeling up to the sky, its string somehow caught the girl's neck from behind and snatched the wig from her head. A few people across from us saw what happened and laughed. I was going to laugh too, until I saw Nathaniel hurriedly pick up the wig and literally slap it back on her head. He did not laugh or smile; he came to her rescue.

I learned a powerful lesson at that moment: Do not mock someone else's misfortune. That very same girl ended up coming into the corner drug store while I was there one day after the episode on the playground. Both of us had our hair in ponytails and she pulled mine. I pulled her hair, in turn, which came off in my hand. We stared at each other for a moment because I did not realize it was her ponytail, at first. I handed it back to her and she stuck it back in the rubber band on her head.

I am still grateful to Nathaniel for teaching me that earlier lesson because I never laughed at her nor the misfortune of others.

Perhaps Nathaniel was innately considerate or perhaps it was our own misfortunes that prompted his thoughtfulness and taught me many life lessons, like that day at the playground. I am not sure I will ever know, because my siblings never really talked to me about how they were feeling. But I knew our father's abandonment and distance was as hard for Nathaniel and Del as it was for me. So, why was Nathaniel the only one whose mind betrayed him? I will never forget standing outside of our house on Churchill that summer day the police came for Nathaniel after one such betrayal of his mind.

I can still see the crowd gathering outside as the police got out of their cars and headed into our house. Nathaniel was on summer break after his second year at Juilliard. I never learned the specific details of that day, but vividly remember Nathaniel's extremely psychotic behavior and Mom reluctantly calling the police.

Nathaniel walked out of the house in handcuffs and looked down at me where I stood on our driveway, next to the porch. His glazed, lost eyes met mine, and they hauled him away.

It was the first time I had seen Nathaniel taken away by the police, and I could not understand why he had to be in handcuffs. Though the police had Nathaniel in handcuffs, they did not need to force him to go. They seemed as bewildered as me about how they had to handle the situation.

It was excruciating to see my brother that way, and I cried all night thinking, "How can this stranger be my brother? Whatever happened to my brother's smile?" I was young when this happened, but I hoped they were treating him well, wherever he was, and prayed God would surround him with kind and merciful people.

I have often wondered if our biological father's abandonment of us and the blended family dynamics with the Mangrums caused Nathaniel's mind to change. I have always wanted to know but cannot bring myself to ask him.

It took some time for me to change the way I viewed the events of that terrible day. Those memories do not haunt me anymore, but I will never forget. Seeing Nathaniel in handcuffs and later in a straight jacket had a profound effect on me.

It Isn't Always Easy

Donald Boone came into my life when I was about 24 years old, after Mom and Alexander Mangrum divorced. The funny thing about that was the great friendship between my mom, Donald, and Alexander. Alexander would visit Mom and Donald (whom we came to call "Dad") now and then, and interestingly, Alexander's respect for Mom increased. Donald Boone was also well-respected, and for some reason, Alexander revered him, immensely. My brother and Donald, however, had a rocky relationship. I am not sure why he and Nathaniel had such harsh run-ins, because Donald was always nice and tried hard to be as supportive as he could with a situation he did not fully understand. Donald was a great man.

I remember Donald would get up early in the winter and drive to Mom's beauty shop to shovel snow and turn the heat on, so the sidewalks would be clear and the shop warm for Mom when she arrived. He was constantly checking on her, bringing her lunch to the shop, and helping around the shop, in general. Donald grew vegetables in his garden, and I could not wait to get my hands on that first bowl of home-made veggie soup.

Donald offered to drive me to and from work once when my car was in the shop for several days. He showed up one morning, and I explained his chauffeuring days were over because the shop had finished repairs on my car. He responded, "Are you sure?" I knew he had not minded taking me, and then I realized he had been enjoying our time together as much as I had been. He would confide in me the overwhelming pride he felt for Mom, his deep hope Nathaniel would get better, and sadness with never knowing how to help Nathaniel. I know Donald prayed for my brother, daily. Mom and Donald allowed Nathaniel to live in their basement, but for reasons I never figured out, Nathaniel simply never liked Donald.

Nathaniel used to write on the walls while he lived in Mom and Donald's basement, but Mom never seemed upset by it. Mom and Dad learned Nathaniel would disappear every now and then and be gone for a while, often weeks at a time. During Nathaniel's absence, Mom would clean the basement, including scrubbing off Nathaniel's writing where she could and would repaint what she could not. Her patience and endurance eventually inspired Dad to join in the effort and he helped her make needed repairs to the basement. Basically, Mom gave Nathaniel a fresh start each time he returned home. I never understood why they went to all that trouble to make repairs until I heard Mom tell Dad she wanted Nathaniel to know she "had not given up on him." How powerful is that?

In retrospect, I believe this season in Nathaniel's life may have been the hardest one for Mom. Nathaniel started taking walks and his writings, previously confined to the basement walls, made their way to public sidewalks. His new, bizarre behavior also included carving on trees and showing up to my job. He would loudly announce to the office staff he was "looking for Jennifer Ayers." I admit, I was a little embarrassed by this, at first, and did not know how to react. It happened often, and Nathaniel never needed anything; he just wanted to see me, though I did not realize that, initially. Eventually, I asked my supervisor, Ms. Vinson, for advice.

Ms. Vinson recounted a job interview her own brother had once gone on to become a hospital physician. I thought she was telling me this story about her brother to recommend his physician services to Nathaniel. She said her brother got the job but unfortunately, he was not a doctor. She shared some of her brother's mental illness struggles with me. I was surprised by her story, but it gave me hope for the first time since Nathaniel's diagnosis. She helped me realize there were other people outside of our family who understood what we were going through. "Just go out there and be his sister," she told me.

The next time Nathaniel came to my office I went out to the lobby and gave him a big hug. I will never forget the smile on his face. I invited him to stay for lunch and we ate together in the cafeteria. I consciously changed my behavior toward him, everyone else at work became more welcoming, and Nathaniel became less boisterous when he arrived. Our office security came to recognize who

Nathaniel was, why he was there and on occasion, they would walk him up to the counter, so he could ask for me. I know my brother appreciated being treated with some respect, compassion, and a little more understanding. The change in my attitude was good for my brother and even better for me. His behavior, however, continued to grow more erratic the older he got. The changes in his behavior were painfully clear one Mother's Day at our grandmother's house.

  I had driven to our grandmother's house with my younger sister, Landi (Kym), in tow. I wanted to take Grandmother the card and gift I had bought for her. She was so happy we thought of her and greeted us with love. We were in the kitchen talking when someone knocked on the door. It was Nathaniel. He had walked all the way there to give Grandmother a card he had gotten for her. We did not tell him we were going to Grandmother's, so he was shocked to see us there.

  I could tell he was upset with me when he realized he had walked all that way (although he walked everywhere) and lost the card he had gotten for Granny. He became irate when he discovered the card for Grandmother was not in his pocket. He screamed terrible things at me, ripping my soul to shreds and leaving me suddenly so ill that I passed out on Grandmother's kitchen floor. My Aunt Martha assumed I passed out from low blood sugar and gave me some orange juice to drink. I never told her it was not diabetes, but the force of

Nathaniel's fury which had made me feel weak and sick. He had frightened everyone, so Aunt Martha lashed back out at Nathaniel to protect us. Her response demonstrated how we all felt; we did not know what to do. The fear we all felt morphed into anger, because we were reacting to something we simply could not understand.

Responding to anger with anger is a natural, human response triggered by the need to protect ourselves. So, it was easy to lash back out at Nathaniel then, because we did not yet know how to deal with him in situations where schizophrenia would prompt an explosive rage from my brother, terrifying those of us on the receiving end. We did not know in the earlier years of his illness whether his rage would stop with his words or progress into physical violence towards us. He did not become physically violent with us that day at Grandmother's, but his words cut us to the bone. In hindsight, I realize, though, that even though my brother had hurt us, he had been hurt by us most of all.

Nathaniel had wanted to do something nice for our grandmother. It was a long walk for him to deliver his grandmother's card only to find his sisters had not invited him along with them. I vividly remember the pain in my brother's face and the fear in everyone else's like it was yesterday. He was already feeling alienated because of schizophrenia, the missing invitation from his sisters probably devastated him, and the lack of understanding from his family completely obliterated him. We eventually learned how to deal with Nathaniel in situations like that, and more time and experience helped us understand that those with a mental health condition may not be able to control their behavior the way we can. This is something everyone needs to understand. I feel even worse today, because I completely understand how his sweet, sentimental act for Grandmother seemed ruined by a lost card, the feeling of being left out, and he could not explain his response to any of it. The pain on his face that day is seared into my mind's eye. The stark realization for me that day was that I was beginning to feel fragile.

It seemed I was always trying to help everyone else hold it together and by this time, Nathaniel was becoming resistant to help. I took a long, hard look at my life. It felt like I was at a dead end and not living for me. Although I had started a greeting card and graphic design business, it was not enough. Some friends of mine had moved to Atlanta and were encouraging me to make a change. Mom and I were close, so I shared with her my urge to do something different with my life in an attempt to figure me out. She reluctantly encouraged me to make the move to Atlanta and offered her support. She said she wanted me to pursue my dreams, even if I was not entirely sure what they were. She believed I needed to try to take a chance and follow my heart. She said moving to Atlanta would either get it out of my system or it would truly work for me, and it did; thank the Lord.

I knew my mother loved me, although she was always preoccupied with trying to put things in place for

Nathaniel. It was difficult to leave my mom; my stepdad, Donald; Nathaniel; my sisters; family; and friends, but I finally made the choice to move to Atlanta when I was around 27 years old. I always had it in the back of my mind I could simply move back home to Cleveland if Mom needed me. Mom and I missed each other terribly when I moved; I had always been her right hand. We talked every day when I first got to Atlanta, but long-distance calls required landline phones back then, and they were expensive. Our costly calls tapered down to weekly, then monthly, then eventually we called on an "as needed" basis. Nathaniel never let my being in Atlanta stop his calls to me from wherever he had traveled to when he needed my help or to talk. Aunt Ollie, a best friend to me by this time, also moved to Atlanta; that was such a happy blessing.

Aunt Ollie needed me to help her clean house and cut her grass, which I was happy to do. After I finished a job, we would sit for hours, while she told me stories about my mother's family. Her stories opened a whole new side of them to me. I loved hearing about what her, my mother, and the rest of my family's lives had been like.

We spent years together before I realized Ollie believed Nathaniel's illness was the result of someone slipping drugs into his drink at a party. That is not how he became ill, of course. Mom and I dealt with Nathaniel's mental illness every day for years, so we took for granted the knowledge we learned about who Nathaniel really was and his daily battle with schizophrenia. It was disappointing to me, in many ways, how little Aunt Ollie and other family members knew about Nathaniel and his mental health condition. I wished they would have striven to understand, too, and then someone could have helped me to make sense of it. I realize now that everyone was doing the best they could, at that time, and lack of understanding was a big issue for everyone.

Personal experience and my work as an advocate in the mental health community has helped me realize how common this scenario is: too often, there is a lack of sincere, diligent effort to understand mental illness for our loved ones who suffer from it, and that creates a tremendous burden to overcome once understanding has finally been achieved. That is another reason my stepdad, Donald Boone – one of the greatest men I have ever known, was a blessed addition to our lives. He never stopped trying to understand my brother, and he always helped Mom.

After living in Atlanta for a while, I would go back to Cleveland, occasionally, for visits. I got word that Donald had been hospitalized because of a horrendous accident that had happened while he was working in his beloved vegetable garden. I flew out to Cleveland at once. He went through months of rehabilitation before ending up in a nursing home. Mom shared with me what had happened.

Mom told me Dad had created a bonfire to burn the leaves and other debris he raked up. He picked up a gas can that was sitting near the fire, and it exploded on him. Panic and shock had prohibited him from yelling for help, but luckily, Mom glanced out the kitchen window and saw Dad frantically trying to put the fire out which was consuming his body. She ran outside with blankets to help Dad and got him to "stop, drop and roll" to extinguish the flames. Mom told me "I didn't have any blankets downstairs. God put those blankets in my hands." The explosion caused debilitating third degree burns over most of Dad's body of which his hands got the worst.

During one of my visits to him in the hospital, Dad showed me where the keys in his pocket had burned through his clothing to his skin leaving a permanent imprint. Mom was visibly shaken sitting in the same seat she had the day of the accident, looking out the kitchen window, and reliving that moment. I tried to change the subject, because I could see the memory of that day still weighed heavily on her mind and in her heart. I was terribly shocked and saddened by the whole accident, and it was extremely difficult for me to see Mom's understandable pain dealing with her husband's terrible accident and the mental health of her son. Mom had to bear so much, but I never heard her complain. She simply kept pushing forward. I returned to my life in Atlanta and months later got word Mom had a stroke.

I flew to Cleveland right after I received the news, connected with my sister, Del, and we went to the hospital to see Mom. Her speech was a little slurred, and she was so cold lying in the bed. I was angry, because they had transferred Mom wearing nothing but a hospital gown – in Cleveland, Ohio! I asked the nurse to "please provide Mom with some warm blankets." They did, and the warmth of the blankets seemed to make Mom feel better to the point where she began to talk a little. I will never understand why I had to ask them for blankets. Although I was upset, I chose not to spend time focusing on the way they had mistreated Mom. Instead, I chose to be grateful she had Del and me there to speak up for her – many people do not have any family support. Then we received notification that another transfer was coming that night to her first nursing home in Chagrin. The transfer to Chagrin made me feel more comfortable. It meant she would be closer to Del, and Nathaniel was familiar with the area if he wanted to walk to see her. Mom seemed to feel better at once after we got her settled in her room in the Alzheimer's area of the newer nursing home. That is when we learned Mom was in the beginning stages of dementia.

    I stayed in Cleveland for several days and with each visit, Mom seemed to improve and get stronger. I visited one day, and found Mom sitting alone in her room. I noticed ladies with Alzheimer's sitting in the hallways loudly talking the same way my brother and Ms. Powell sometimes would. One lady followed me into Mom's room.

Mom gave her a stern look and politely waved the woman out. The lady left without a word. Mom said to me "to be understood, you have to know how to communicate to let them know you understand." I was surprised because she had spoken clearly and was showing her concern about someone else, once again. She did not want the lady to feel badly or unwanted, yet she knew she had to stand her ground. The next day, I had to leave and head back to Atlanta, as much as I did not want to leave. I felt bad leaving Del to oversee everything, and I am grateful for all the sacrifices she made with her time checking on Mom and Dad. I did fly back for Mom's next birthday, though.

 Del and I threw a little birthday party in the front lobby of the nursing home. I remember the look Mom and Aunt Ollie shared when they finally saw each other again after such an exceedingly long stretch of time; it still touches my heart. They were always so close and had never had to endure such a long season of separation. I had nicknamed them "the snoop sisters," because that is what they did. They thought their nickname was funny. Aunt Ollie walked up to Mom in the lobby and looked her in the eyes. I could see Aunt Ollie was nervous about Mom remembering her. Aunt Ollie prepared herself then said, "Flo, do you know who I am?" Mom shook her head no saying, "Uh Uh," and Aunt Ollie hung her head. Mom started laughing then replied, "Ollie." They both laughed which perked up Aunt Ollie right away. Many people came for Mom's party including aunts, uncles, grandchildren, great grandchildren, cousins, and a few friends – many of whom are no longer with us.

    Mom smiled and was happy to see everyone who came to her party but did not talk much. Her smiles disappeared after a few minutes as she got lost in her thoughts. She looked so sad watching others mingle. I leaned over and quietly asked, "What's wrong, Mom?" She said, as she looked at me with sad eyes, "Where's Tony? I miss Tony." It was a painful moment for both of us, because her bad health and inability to communicate as she once had done did not stop her from saying, "Where's Tony?" Looking back on that time, I wanted to believe Nathaniel would visit Mom, but wisdom sadly reminds me how the facility would have treated him, most likely not very welcoming, had he tried to visit. I have looked back on this time often wondering what I could have done differently.

    I asked Mom if I should move back to Cleveland. Her response was, "For what? Stay where you are!" Mom never wanted to prohibit others from walking out their own, unique path or pursuing their own dreams. Her encouragement set me free to continue building my life in Atlanta where I was striving to be successful in my career, in my relationships with my adopted children, and with Jerry who would later become my husband. I got the impression that she felt like staying in Atlanta was best for me rather than uprooting my family by moving to Cleveland. Jerry's support for me, especially during this timeframe, was a Godsend. Jerry supplied much needed joy, encouragement, stability, and wisdom to our family as things continued to grow more challenging for Mom, Dad and Nathaniel. A month after Mom's party, Del moved her to the same nursing home as Dad. That made Dad extremely happy.

    Mom and Dad got to be in the same room for a while which was a blessing for them both. Eventually, they had to move Mom to a different floor, because she started behaving like the ladies with Alzheimer's from her previous nursing home. Her regression was difficult for me to watch. Distance from Mom and the bleak diagnosis that he would never get better could not keep Dad away though. It was as though he willed himself to get better so he could wheel himself to Mom's side in a different room on a different floor. Why did he do this? So, he could do the only thing for Mom he was able to do; hold her hand.

    Through closed eyes, Mom would hold out her hand waiting to feel Dad's touch. The nursing staff on Dad's floor knew his daily mission, and always helped him prepare to see Mom. I was a witness one day to this beautiful act of love. Dad took Mom's hand and tenderly said, "Hi Flo. I'm here." And on that day, God allowed me to see Mom smile. The blessing of that day is a gift I will forever cherish. But she continued to deteriorate.

    The last time I saw Mom alive, she was bedridden, had a feeding tube, and seemed lifeless. The memory of that day still makes me feel sick. Mom was not moving, so I sat right beside her and laid my head on her hand. I said, "Mom, this is Jenny, I love you. Are you comfortable?" I wanted her to hear my voice and know I was there. "I love you, Momma. Momma, I love you." I stayed by her side for about four hours. I got up to leave and said once more, "I love you, Momma." She opened her eyes then opened and closed her hand. I believe she was telling me she knew I was there. Mom was sick from the stroke and in a nursing home for nearly a year before she died in August of 2000. I wish I could have sung 500 Miles to her, one last time. I am so grateful Jerry got the chance to meet Mom on another visit before she died. Jerry and Joshua traveled back to Cleveland with me to attend the beautiful home going service Del had arranged for Mom.

Losing Mom was tough for me since I was living in Atlanta and regretted not being by her side to help as often as I would have liked. I know it was even tougher on my sister, Del, because she was the one who took care of everything in my absence. I believe Mom's stroke, sickness, and death was toughest for Nathaniel though, even though he was in the same city as Mom. He was not well at all during this time and his own struggles prohibited him from helping anyone. Mom's death robbed Nathaniel of his refuge, and we could not find him anywhere as we prepared for her funeral. I knew I needed to go drive around to look for Nathaniel to tell him about Mom and make sure he was okay.

I found Nathaniel at the corner of Chagrin and Lee Road. I did not know where I would take him; I just wanted to rescue him from wandering the streets for as long as he would allow, even if just for a moment. I yelled, "Anthony," and waved him over to my car. He waved me away with a hurt, angry look, so I knew he was already aware Mom had died. Of all the things I have seen my brother go through, I can say with certainty this was the hardest to watch. We must all leave this earth some point, but it does not make it any easier to lose a loved one — especially losing a loving parent like our mother — and filtering that loss through the lens of mental illness. It was difficult for me to lose our mother, but I had been a witness to her suffering and knew she was finally at peace. But as far as I knew, my brother had not seen her pain, nor could he reconcile in his mind she was no longer suffering. It seemed he was just angry about her not being there.

My heart ached seeing Nathaniel's pain that day, and I worried terribly at what he might do. I knew I could not help him if he would not let me; I cried myself to sleep that night. I prayed he would come to Mom's "homegoing" service, but he did not. I had longed to have the chance to talk through his grief with him and encourage him to learn how to carry on, but he did not give me the chance. Not having our mother around to support him seemed to further his decline and he shut everyone out completely for a very long time. The long road we had traveled became arduous and the daunting task of keeping track of my brother became nearly impossible.

    Nathaniel was MIA. Mom was gone. Then one day, I heard Nathaniel had gone to Los Angeles.

To Treat or Not to Treat

My brother, Nathaniel, has never been excited by the prospect of any mental health treatment, let alone inpatient treatment. The idea of hospitalization is not appealing to most individuals, but that does not change the need for it. For Nathaniel, the thought of being inside his own apartment with freedom to come and go as he pleases is, at times, hard to swallow, so the thought of being forced into a controlled, monitored, treatment facility is unthinkable.

Nathaniel once screamed at me, "There is nothing wrong with me!" when he thought I was making a trip to see him only to force him into a mental health treatment facility. His inability to recognize when his behavior is becoming erratic and dangerous leads him to conclude we are being unnecessarily cruel when we suggest or force him into treatment. The first time I realized Nathaniel, most likely, needed to be forced into a treatment facility was during his turbulent college years when the illness really began to manifest.

Nathaniel attended his freshman year of college at Ohio University in 1969 on a full ride music scholarship. In 1970, he chose to attend The Juilliard School in New York, however, since he had auditioned and been accepted on a full ride scholarship while he was still attending Ohio University. Nathaniel's summer break between Ohio University and Juilliard meant change for our entire family as we tried to adapt to the "episodes" that began to manifest in Nathaniel.

My brother had not shown any manifestation of mental illness until he went to Juilliard. The obvious episodes of mental illness came after he attended Juilliard. We knew he was sick, and something was wrong, but did not know to call it schizophrenia. I hurt so much for my brother. My emotions felt trapped in a bottle with the lid on too tight allowing no release for my pain. Then Mom began to search for serious help after we picked Nathaniel up for the summer break before his junior year at Juilliard. My brother did not show any manifestation of mental illness until he went to Juilliard, the obvious episodes of mental illness came after he attended Juilliard.

Mom, Alexander Mangrum, and I had driven to New York to pick up Nathaniel for summer break after that second year at Juilliard. I was excited, and the drive there was full of joyous anticipation. We were caught off guard, though, when Nathaniel came out to the car. His disheveled appearance and erratic behavior were a devastating sight. The expression on Mom's face conveyed exactly how I felt.

I did not know what to say to Mom nor Nathaniel, so I closed my eyes and pretended to sleep on the way home. I would occasionally peek at Mom through squinted eyes to see how she was coping with Nathaniel's incoherent ramblings. She stared directly at the road in front of her trying desperately to stay involved in the conversation with my brother, but I could see her pain. None of us had expected him to be so ill – especially not with a mental health disorder.

Schizophrenia was clearly manifesting in my brother, and there was no way to deny he was changing. The feeling of the trip had abruptly shifted, but Alexander tried to keep his attitude upbeat which helped lift our heavy mood making the long journey home to Cleveland more bearable.

Nathaniel stayed in Cleveland the summer of 1971 before returning to Juilliard for his junior year. Unfortunately, his grades declined that school year from straight A's, and he had a breakdown during winter break. Mom had to pick Nathaniel up from a psychiatric hospital in New York. He had gotten into a confrontation with some of his housemates and they felt threatened. I have never felt threatened by my brother, but I understand other's trepidation.

Interacting with someone like Nathaniel can be scary for those not accustomed to the unpredictable reactions and behavior of those suffering from mental health disorders. Sadly, many do not want to take the necessary time required to personally know and understand those with a mental health condition. Instead, people are content to believe what they hear in the news about the mentally ill which is usually a stigmatizing story about someone snapping and hurting themselves or others.

Those stories initially breed fear, misunderstanding, and a frenzied outcry for mental health awareness. Once the sensationalized horror of such a story wears off, isolation begins again for the mental health community. People carry on with deep-seeded, fear-laden stereotypes of the mentally ill, no one is better off, and the mentally ill continue to suffer.

That was true for Nathaniel considering that break down ended his time at Juilliard, and his episodes increased after that. And, it was not the last time Nathaniel would have a run-in with roommates who did not try to understand him.

Nathaniel had been the lead/principal bassist for The Ohio State University orchestra when Mom and I went to watch him perform, once, in a Christmas concert. Nathaniel gave us a tour of the school before the concert which ended in a visit to his room under the football stadium. Nathaniel introduced us to his roommate, a white OSU football player, by stating in a calm, matter of fact way, "He has a mean punch! Clocked me right in my jaw the other day!"

Nathaniel's tall, muscular roommate watched for our reaction to my brother's statement. I could see the guilty look in that guy's eyes, and I felt as sick as if I had been the one punched. I could not fathom why he would hurt my brother. But I have learned over the years that fear of the unknown makes it easier for people to be mean and spiteful to people with a mental health condition. I felt like I was in a nightmare and instantly regretted not retaliating by socking the football player in the jaw. He made Nathaniel look like a shrimp, so it was clear Nathaniel posed no threat to that bully. The thought of how he had hurt my brother physically and mentally made me want to cry; it still does.

Nathaniel's roommate was a perfect example of how mean people can be, and the mentally ill understand this type of cruelty even less than you or I do. I chose to contain myself in the moment for two reasons. Firstly, I did not want to make it worse for Nathaniel because he had to live with that guy after Mom and I went home. Secondly, I knew a thumping from me would not fix my brother's roommate problem.

Mom told Nathaniel to let us know when things like that happened to him, but I do not think he had anyone he could turn to at The Ohio State University. I struggled with that moment almost every day for years until this scripture in Romans 12:19-21 helped me move on: "Dearly beloved, avenge not yourselves, but rather give place unto wrath: for vengeance is mine; I will repay, saith the Lord."

Now I hope Nathaniel's OSU roommate reads this book and has matured enough to apologize for violently overacting to his own fear and lack of understanding of mental illness when he was in no real danger from his smaller, weaker roommate – Nathaniel. Though my brother appears on the surface to have let this incident go years ago, I am certain an apology would help heal a part of him still wounded from that incident. The concert turned out to be amazing after we got over the initial roommate unpleasantness.

Nathaniel played the bass beautifully and received a roaring standing ovation. We went backstage after the concert was over to find him in a peculiar tuxedo three sizes too large, standing in a daze as people showered him with congratulations on his fabulous performance. He would momentarily snap out of the daze to shake his head or mumble a thank you.

Mom was so proud of him, but Nathaniel did not reciprocate the hug she tried to give him. We took him out for a celebratory dinner afterwards. He seemed a bit better at dinner, but he was still strangely distant. I was worried about my brother as we drove home to Cleveland, and rightfully so. Nathaniel disappeared from school. Unfortunately, it was not the last time he would vanish.

Mom called around, frantically trying to find Nathaniel. My cousin James, a police officer in Columbus, helped Mom by looking for my brother, but his search was unsuccessful. Nathaniel eventually came home to Cleveland, tired and weary. He chose not to stay at that university which I was glad about considering the abuse he had endured at the hands of his roommate. Despite suffering a breakdown, abuse, and rejection at the hands of his college roommates, Nathaniel never gave up. He continued to pursue music and to further his music education. He was accepted wherever he applied. Not only did he attend The Juilliard School, Ohio University, and the Ohio State University, but Case Western Reserve University also accepted him. He also attended The Aspen Colorado Music Festivals and played Senior Centers and churches until he was simply not well enough to do so anymore.

    Deep down, I knew what had to happen after watching my brother's decline. One way or another, Nathaniel needed hospitalization or some sort of mental health treatment facility. I had hoped he would go willingly, but we soon discovered that would not be the case and he was getting worse.

    Nathaniel's increased episodes brought with them more hospital and mental institution stays than I can count or even remember. No one seemed to be able to help him. Nathaniel's hospitalizations triggered strife in his relationships with Mom and me. He would eventually calm down and welcome us into his presence, but each time was traumatic for us all. I was involved in almost every situation where my brother became hospitalized before I went off to college.

    I made a sincere effort to support Mom as she sought help for my brother. I think we both believed Nathaniel would miraculously transform back to the person we knew before he became ill if we could find the right help. I would ask Nathaniel to voluntarily go to the hospital to get help, but his varied experiences with all sorts of treatments made him wary. I am sure it never seemed like help to him, rather it seemed like torture, especially after he had endured shock treatment (ECT – Electroconvulsive Therapy.)

    Mom was so hopeful at the prospect of how shock treatment could help Nathaniel. Statistically, we knew ECT's potential therapeutic effect could have given my brother his life back. We never wanted to hurt Nathaniel. We wanted to do everything we could to help him be okay. Mom and I sat in the small waiting room of the doctor's office waiting for Nathaniel to tell us how his first shock treatment went. Mom was nervous, and I vividly remember Nathaniel visibly shaking as he exited the treatment room with his eyes as big as saucers. The doctors looked at us in a very unfriendly manner and Mom hung her head.

    I fought to keep from crying in the back seat of our car on the way home as I wondered, "why is this happening?" Nathaniel was distant after that and reluctant to seek out help. Consequently, I was a party to Mom's visits to Probate Court at City Hall where Nathaniel was legally committed to court-ordered, involuntary hospitalizations meant to protect and help him.

    I often went to visit Nathaniel during his hospitalizations. Too often the medications he received in those facilities made him lethargic and zombie-like. He seemed to consistently respond to the medication in the same way, no matter how nice the facility was. It was always difficult to see him that way. He was glad to see me when I visited, even though the medications kept him from staying mentally present during my visits. He came to expect my visits though, and during one of his hospitalizations he announced to his nurses I was coming to see him.

    The nurses told me my brother spoke of me often, and his assurance of my visits made me glad. I remember noting on that visit how Nathaniel was no longer the dapper, well-coordinated dresser from our youth. His red sweater could not brighten his glum mood. He asked me to bring his bass and some music to him, but the facility prohibited it.

    I broke the news to Nathaniel and felt terrible as I watched him grow even more morose. I acutely felt how lonely he must have been in that dark place. He never wanted me to go when I needed to leave, and he would strike up conversations about anything to get me to stay, just as he does now.

    I know Nathaniel grew to hate the medication during those times of forced hospitalizations where he was separated from his family and denied a musical outlet. He was unable to physically hear the music because they had taken away his instruments, and he was unable to hear the music in his mind because of the sensory deadening pharmaceuticals in his body. Medication does seem to help

Nathaniel, but the experiences that took away his ability to hear the music still convince him otherwise.

Some people judge the decisions my family had to make about Nathaniel's care as cruel but that has never been the case. I have missed my brother, terribly, during the many years he spent in treatment facilities, on the streets of Los Angeles, on Skid Row, or dropping off the map to travel across the country. Not knowing and sometimes even knowing where my brother was has been equally heart-wrenching and has elicited more hours praying for his well-being than I could ever tally.

Looking at our situation from the outside in may make you wonder if we really loved or genuinely cared for my brother. I can say with emphatic certainty that our family has always loved Nathaniel and tried to help him the best we knew how. Only those dealing with a loved one suffering from mental illness, particularly schizophrenia, can understand our journey. My plea is for families going through this struggle to receive support rather than judgment as they try to survive the lifelong journey through mental illness. The tumultuous journey requires patience, education, and growth from the mentally ill and family, alike, and can sometimes feel like navigating quicksand.

It took many years for me to realize there is a line not to cross when trying to help a mentally ill loved one. I imagine other families have discovered that line too. I desperately wanted my brother to be "well" – "normal" like everyone else. It was difficult watching my brother go from my hero before his illness to a stranger I did not recognize after his illness. I did not always understand him then, and I still struggle to this day. I kept living in the past and fantasized about the day we would find the magic treatment, which would give me my brother back and give Nathaniel his life back. I had to learn that living in the past was robbing me of the present with my brother.

Nathaniel had developed a new vision for himself and my attempt to make him who he used to be – who I wanted him to be – crossed the line. A line, that never should have been crossed. It was not easy, but I came to embrace the fact Nathaniel is the man he is going to be. I opened my heart to my brother. We shared, listened, and grew which enabled us to help many others grow.

As for those with a mental health condition, they might think it is the rest of us who are the problem and not them. They may have a point.

"There is a line not to cross when trying to help a mentally ill loved one."

My "Iron Sharpens Iron" Marriage

Jerry and I first met on Browns Mill golf course in Atlanta in 1998. We had seen each other on many occasions, and for the longest time had shared nothing more than a love for golf and a "hello." He reminded me of the actor and comedian, Sinbad, when I first saw him, especially because I could see he was a very funny guy and God knew I needed a laugh at that time.

It took me a while to ask anyone about Jerry's relationship status, but I became intrigued after I walked by him one day and turned back for a second look to see he had also turned back to look at me! We were gazing at each other, clearly caught by our second glances, when he raised an eyebrow and gave me a nod. I asked someone at the course, "Is he married?" She responded, "No." One could say I was interested.

I was playing a round at Browns Mill with a friend in April of 1998 and saw Jerry playing ahead of us. He realized I was playing behind him. Rather than going to the clubhouse at the turn, he waited for my partner and I to catch up and asked, "Are y'all playing the back?" My friend, Robin the matchmaker, said, "Y'all should play the back." Jerry responded, "I'm good with that," so he and I set out to play the back nine together. I was playing well at the time, and he was extremely complimentary of my game. We had so much fun playing together several times a week after that. He would set up games for us with his friends, and he especially got a kick out of watching me beat his friend, Bobby.

Uncle Nathaniel, hanging out with his nephews, Duane and Joshua, nearly 25 years ago. They admired their uncle even though they were too young to fully understand him. My son, Joshua, had a deeper understanding because of how close I was with Nathaniel.

Jerry was not only fun and my best friend, but he was supportive of me and my family. Jerry really welcomed getting to know my 8-year-old, adopted son, Joshua. I had also adopted an older boy, but he was in college and never around much when Jerry and I started dating. He went to the Navy after college and got reacquainted with his biological family. I am sincerely happy he had the opportunity to reconnect with them. Jerry was extremely close to his two biological children and two stepchildren from a previous marriage. I feel blessed that I was able to develop a good relationship with one of his children, Stephanie, and her mother, Cathy.

Jerry helped my relationship with Nathaniel. I had existed in a perpetual state of hurt with my brother for years and did not know how to function outside of the pain I felt over my brother's plight in life. Jerry taught me how to laugh and recognize the humorous side of my brother which set our relationship free in some ways. Jerry was a tough guy to his friends, but he was our big teddy bear at home. He did not talk much, but he boldly pushed me to pursue my dreams.

When Jerry would see me getting stressed out and stalled by the details of whatever project I was pursuing, he would simply say, "Just do it!" like it was not a big deal. He helped me to get out of my head and keep pushing forward, no matter what. He was incredibly supportive and proud of me every time I would write poetry, short stories, or even created presentations for work or family. He would have pushed me toward finishing this book if he were still with me by saying, "Just do it!"

Jerry began developing symptoms of kidney failure and growing increasingly sick after we first began dating. I was extremely worried about him, and even though we were not married yet, I stepped in to help him get the care he needed since his doctor was dragging his feet. After much heartache and fighting for treatment, we discovered his kidney was only functioning at 10% which required a kidney transplant in 2003 – 5 years after we met.

Seven years later, I decided to hold a surprise birthday party dinner for Jerry's 60th at the golf course we frequented. Jerry only knew we were going to dinner with some of my friends, which he was always up for since he was a big ham and enjoyed being the life of the party. I came home to fetch him and found him lying in bed not feeling well at all. I had used several people to create an elaborate scheme to throw him off the scent of a surprise party, but I offered to cancel dinner once I saw how badly he felt.

Jerry insisted we go to dinner anyway, so reluctantly, we did. I knew he was not being himself, but I genuinely had no idea how sick he truly was. He was surprised and it turned out to be a nice party. I was worried the whole time though, because he never once moved from his chair that propped him up against the wall. That was completely out of character for him, considering he was a talker and liked to joke around. It seemed he was waiting for the last guest to leave before he passed out, collapsing to the floor. We learned that the transplanted kidney had failed, and his diabetes made navigating a second round of kidney failure even more tricky, desensitizing him to pain – especially in his feet. He had to begin peritoneal dialysis, once again. He seemed to improve for only about a year before he ended up in the hospital.

I had been working one evening in April of 2011, teaching an evening class, and came home to find Jerry had severe burns on his feet from soaking his feet in scalding water that he could not feel. I almost hyperventilated from the severity of the wounds and begged him to let me take him to the emergency room. He absolutely refused to go and insisted he would see his doctor the next day. I helplessly acquiesced, and the next morning he once again insisted, "I am not in any pain. You go to work. I can take care of myself." I went to work and told my manager I might have to leave to help Jerry. Jerry called me later saying we needed to go to the hospital at the suggestion of his doctor and that is where he spent his final 6 months of life, except for 5 days.

Jerry was in pain during those many months, but I always held out hope he was coming home and prepared the house to make it easier for him once he did come home. I did everything I could to make him comfortable those 5 days he spent at home, but he was 6'5" and 230 pounds, so I was not strong enough to help him by myself. Jerry knew he had to return to the hospital, even though he did not want to go. I had become exhausted during this time, and Jerry's siblings were wonderful with helping.

Jerry's sister, Jacqueline, intuitively had a knack for showing up exactly when we needed her. His sister, Eula, and his brother, Kofi, would always make themselves available when I needed to conduct out-of-town presentations. Eula visited Jerry in the hospital and sometimes spent the night. I can never thank them enough for their support. In fact, I know I would not have made it through had it not been for Eula; I cannot emphasize enough how grateful I am that she was always there. I used to wish my brother had the type of support Jerry had in his family, but really, Jerry's family were supportive of Nathaniel.

A few of Jerry's siblings would visit Nathaniel when they made journeys to California. I remember Jerry's sister, Melanie, was in California for business once and sacrificed time in her schedule to drive to Skid Row in Los Angeles to take Nathaniel to lunch. That visit was a big deal, and I remember Nathaniel calling to me to tell me every detail.

In his final months, Jerry would take calls from my brother on the days he felt well enough to interact with Nathaniel, which was not always easy. Jerry never told my brother he was in the hospital. I knew he was trying to protect Nathaniel. Those conversations sometimes distracted Jerry and Nathaniel, both, from their respective battles long enough for laughter to ensue; I still cherish that sweet sound. I do not know how Jerry, nor I, would have for the last guest to leave before he passed out, collapsing to the floor. We learned that the transplanted kidney had failed, and his diabetes made navigating a second round of kidney failure even more tricky, desensitizing him to pain – especially in his feet. He had to begin peritoneal dialysis, once again. He seemed to improve for only about a year before he ended up in the hospital.

    I had been working one evening in April of 2011, teaching an evening class, and came home to find Jerry had severe burns on his feet from soaking his feet in scalding water that he could not feel. I almost hyperventilated from the severity of the wounds and begged him to let me take him to the emergency room. He absolutely refused to go and insisted he would see his doctor the next day. I helplessly acquiesced, and the next morning he once again insisted, "I am not in any pain. You go to work. I can take care of myself." I went to work and told my manager I might have to leave to help Jerry. Jerry called me later saying we needed to go to the hospital at the suggestion of his doctor and that is where he spent his final 6 months of life, except for 5 days.

    Jerry was in pain during those many months, but I always held out hope he was coming home and prepared the house to make it easier for him once he did come home. I did everything I could to make him comfortable those 5 days he spent at home, but he was 6'5" and 230 pounds, so I was not strong enough to help him by myself. Jerry knew he had to return to the hospital, even though he did not want to go. I had become exhausted during this time, and Jerry's siblings were wonderful with helping.

Jerry's sister, Jacqueline, intuitively had a knack for showing up exactly when we needed her. His sister, Eula, and his brother, Kofi, would always make themselves available when I needed to conduct out-of-town presentations. Eula visited Jerry in the hospital and sometimes spent the night. I can never thank them enough for their support. In fact, I know I would not have made it through had it not been for Eula; I cannot emphasize enough how grateful I am that she was always there. I used to wish my brother had the type of support Jerry had in his family, but really, Jerry's family were supportive of Nathaniel.

A few of Jerry's siblings would visit Nathaniel when they made journeys to California. I remember Jerry's sister, Melanie, was in California for business once and sacrificed time in her schedule to drive to Skid Row in Los Angeles to take Nathaniel to lunch. That visit was a big deal, and I remember Nathaniel calling to me to tell me every detail.

In his final months, Jerry would take calls from my brother on the days he felt well enough to interact with Nathaniel, which was not always easy. Jerry never told my brother he was in the hospital. I knew he was trying to protect Nathaniel. Those conversations sometimes distracted Jerry and Nathaniel, both, from their respective battles long enough for laughter to ensue; I still cherish that sweet sound. I do not know how Jerry, nor I, would have managed this timeframe without his loving, supportive family. Jerry's family was and is simply phenomenal and their support for Jerry and Nathaniel has deeply touched my heart. I cannot find the words to accurately express the depths of my gratitude to Jerry and his family for their help and love.

    I know my experiences sitting in the hospital with Nathaniel and then Jerry helped to prepare me to manage both situations more effectively. The devastating circumstances were completely different, but I had a tremendous amount of practice putting on a smiling, brave face to talk music or whatever else with Nathaniel and to talk about everything else in the world with Jerry, including Nathaniel.

"Bravely shedding light on our battles may embolden another to speak out, get help, and boldly share the beautiful music of their own lives."

My Father

My siblings and I saw little of our biological father after that day in the Cleveland Hopkins airport where he boarded the plane for California to start his new life without us. Years would pass before I would see him again. Our father and his wife never invited me or my sister, Del, to visit them in Los Angeles, but I remember they asked Nathaniel to spend a summer with them once before his schizophrenia diagnosis. He was a young teen, and they sent him home after two weeks claiming he ate too much. I often wonder how things might have been different if our father had been there to help Mom with Nathaniel after his diagnosis. Instead, we got used to our father disappointing us.

I remember being so excited to open a box I received from my father one year on my birthday. My mom saw the excitement on my face turn to disappointment as I gazed at the items inside which included a paper-thin brown and green dress. We rarely spoke, so of course, he would not have known what I liked.

Mom was disgusted and upset and told me I did not have to wear any of it. I know she felt it was her job to protect us from that disappointment. I do not recall my sister ever getting anything from our father or his wife except an argument.

Our father who Nathaniel favors. He was never able to accept that his only son and namesake was sick with a mental health disorder. May he rest in peace.

Our father and his wife had driven through Cleveland with my two half-sisters, once, when I was about thirteen. Nathaniel was not with Del and me when we went to visit our father at Aunt Willa and Uncle Howard's house. I had not seen him in years, yet he had the nerve to ask me if I liked him or my stepfather better. My aunt walked in and stopped the conversation in the nick of time, so I did not have to answer. Then my stepmom and Del ended up in an argument at dinner, so we left without further conversation with them.

    I was 21 years old the next time I saw my father. He and his family had driven from L.A. to Atlanta to attend a family reunion I was also attending. I carpooled from Dayton to Atlanta with family from my father's side and was excited about seeing him. When I finally saw my father after many hours driving and all those years apart, the only thing he said to me was, "You look like your mother." No hello. No hug. No gesture of any kind showing he was happy to see me. I felt crushed and hid in the bathroom to cry. My cousin Sheila comforted me, upset by what she had seen take place between me and my father, her uncle. I avoided him for the rest of the weekend.

    Watching him prepare to leave with the family which had replaced us I thought, "This is the last time I will see my father." I ran off, devastatingly hurt, and exploded in a gut-wrenching cry. Aunt Mattie told him about my bathroom meltdown, so he came to my room. He cared enough to seek me out which shocked me, but I hurt too deeply to open the door when he knocked. I did not believe him when he said through the door, "You can come visit me anytime you want." There was no love in his voice. He slipped a twenty-dollar bill under the door while saying, "I'll see you later." Later turned out to be another twelve years.

My father came to visit me in Atlanta after I reached out to him, asking for his forgiveness. He and I were never close, but I knew I needed to forgive him for my own good. I confessed I had held onto bitterness and unforgiveness toward him for years. I was bitter he split up our family. I was bitter he abandoned Nathaniel when Nathaniel needed him most. I was bitter he moved across the country and forgot about us as he built a new life with a new family. Although I had forgiven him, there was a part of me which needed to hear him say it. He forgave me, of course, but he never apologized for the pain he had caused. While he was visiting me in Atlanta, my father and I attended a church, together, that a friend of his from California had started.

My father introduced me to his friend after church. His friend was surprised to meet me, since he had no idea my father had children other than those in California. It seemed we did not exist to our father when he was in California, a point driven home to me when my father's friend said, "Brother Ayers, I didn't know you had other children." That moment was yet another painful, emotional blow handed to me by my father. I wondered how Del or Nathaniel would have managed that situation. Would either of them have been able to stomach the sight of our father after the cutting confirmation we were out of his sight and mind once he moved to California? I am glad they did not have to endure that. The rest of my father's visit was challenging for me, but I held it together until, once again, he left my life.

Another several years passed before my father asked if he could again visit me in Atlanta. My mother had already died, I was divorced and was raising my two adopted sons. Time had healed my wounds from his earlier visit, and I was ready to reconnect with him. The week before he arrived, he asked if Nathaniel could come along. I spoke with Nathaniel and told him I was eager to have him come stay, and he sounded happy. I knew it was because he had our father back in his life, for the time being. He had always deeply loved our father. Nathaniel seemed in such a good place, I felt it would be a proper time to suggest he get some help while he was visiting me. He did not seem to take my suggestion well.

Worried about Nathaniel's response, I told my father he needed to stay with Nathaniel while in Los Angeles, before their trip to Atlanta. I am not sure what happened but a week later he called to tell me my brother was not coming. He said Nathaniel was staying with our half-sister and doing well, but Nathaniel became homeless not long after that. My father did come to visit me, and what was originally a couple of weeks turned into a few months.

My father seemed happy to be staying with me, my sons, and Jerry. Jerry and I were not married yet when my father came to stay, but Jerry was recuperating at my house after receiving his kidney transplant. My father never mentioned returning home, so I let him stay. I was happy to have him with me, and he helped Jerry tremendously with his recovery. But my father staying with me did cause tension with his wife. I bought a new home in the months he stayed with me, and she always believed he had given me money. He had not, of course. My father told me he returned home to trouble the last time he had stayed with me. Apparently, his wife did not want him to spend time with me.

Out of the blue, (so it seemed) my father received divorce papers at my house. He was 80 years old and his marriage had lasted much longer than the one to my mother. He seemed so surprised by receiving the divorce papers, and I suspect their arrival at my house was meant as a message to me. My stepmother was making it clear where we stood. My father abruptly returned to L.A. and the divorce went through. He ended up in an assisted living facility not long after his return to L.A. and his divorce was finalized.

In 2008, Jerry, now my husband, and I flew to L.A. so I could do an interview with 60 Minutes about Nathaniel. I thought it would be great while I was there to take my brother to see our father at his assisted living facility. Nathaniel was grumpy when we arrived at his apartment which he had gotten through LAMP Mental Health Services. We took him to dinner before we visited our father. Thankfully, his mood lifted by the time dinner was over. He had invited a neighbor who lived in his apartment complex to join us for dinner.

Nathaniel's friend had recently received some upsetting news about his health and was having a tough time. My brother made sure his friend ate that day and took food home with him. I felt enormously proud of Nathaniel for extending such kindness. We stood outside after dinner as I contemplated taking Nathaniel to see our father. I wondered if it might be better to surprise him with our destination, rather than tell him my plans. I was lost in thought when Nathaniel walked over to me and said, "Ok. What are we going to do now?"

"I don't know," I responded, honestly, not knowing what would be best for Nathaniel.

He walked away momentarily, then he approached me again in frustration saying, "Are you a dentist?"

Confused, I replied, "What?"

"Because getting answers out of you is like pulling teeth!" he quipped.

Everyone thought it was funny, except me. I was worried about ruining Nathaniel's recently lifted mood. I did not know how he would respond to visiting our father. Jerry revealed to him our plans to visit our father, and Nathaniel seemed elated. It took us an hour to drive from L.A. to the nice, clean, care facility in Northridge. The residents were just finishing dinner and the place was bustling as one of the facility attendants fetched our father. He looked confused and it seemed he was trying to figure out who Nathaniel and I were, although he knew Jerry right away. He never called me by name, but he did finally say, "Anthony," which made my brother feel better.

    Nathaniel had brought his violin, and I could tell he really wanted to play for our father. Our father saw the violin, but he never asked Nathaniel to play. I am sure my brother did not think about Father's age nor health stifling his etiquette and prohibiting him from asking Nathaniel to play as a courtesy. Knowing Nathaniel was itching to play, we chose to go downstairs so we did not disturb a church group ministering to the residents in the lobby. There was a lot of buzz about Steve Lopez's book, newspaper articles, and the movie, by this point, so people quickly realized who Nathaniel was when he began to play the violin.

    Our father's response to Nathaniel's playing was disheartening. He did not offer one compliment to my brother on his music. Nathaniel was clearly disappointed but tried to stay positive. He stopped playing, looked at Father and reminisced, "I remember you got me a bass that was nice." I was surprised because I never knew our father had supported my brother's music in any way. Nathaniel tried to keep a conversation going with our father and Jerry tried to help Nathaniel in his effort. I listened, trying to take it all in. An uncomfortable silence filled the air. Nathaniel became fidgety. Our father brashly broke the silence with, "What's wrong with him?"

    His audacity shocked me, even though I knew he had never come to terms with his son's illness, always insisting, "Nathaniel could work on it" if he really wanted to get better. Nathaniel quickly responded, "What's wrong with you?"

That was it. Nathaniel was angry and wanted to leave. I was terribly sad as we headed back to the lobby. Nathaniel clutched his violin, itching for pain relief only playing his music could provide. He needed to leave, so we said our goodbyes. Nathaniel was clearly hurting and mumbled under his breath as we drove back to L.A. We needed to stop for gas along the way, and Nathaniel asked for a bottle of water. As if we had not been through enough pain that evening, we had to endure an all too familiar reaction as we entered the gas station to get water for my brother.

I watched from a short distance as a woman rolled her eyes at Nathaniel and almost tripped over her own feet to get away from him. Nathaniel stood there with his drink in one hand, his money in the other and she acted as if she might catch a horrible disease from him. Had his day not been rough enough already without having to be sniped at by this woman? I shifted into defensive mode and charged to my brother's side asking him, "Do you have everything you want?" My presence seemed to reassure the woman that she would be able to escape the likes of my brother, unscathed.

I shared with Steve about the whole visit to see Nathaniel's and my father. I felt badly about how things turned out and that the trip had an unfortunate, negative effect on my brother's behavior for months. I knew how much Nathaniel loved our father and wanted to see him again, but one of the producers for the movie *The Soloist* suggested to Steve and me that we refrain from such visits for a time. Though I had often wondered if Nathaniel would have been better with our father's presence in his life, that moment between Nathaniel and our father helped me realize his presence could have made Nathaniel worse.

    Our father simply could not understand that Nathaniel was sick. I prayed about the producer's suggestion and agreed to hold off on visits to our father for a while considering all the publicity Nathaniel was receiving from the movie, and more importantly, he needed time to heal. It was such an emotionally challenging time for me too that I began to get the same "out of body" feeling I got as a child when extremely stressful situations arose. I was physically present but felt like my mind was looking down from outside of my body. There may be a diagnosis for me too, I suppose.

Everything Changes, Again

On April 14, 2005, I received a call from Steve Lopez that started a chain reaction of change in Nathaniel's life, forever. I had not heard from my brother since the death of our mother, five years prior. Nathaniel's voice simply washed me over me, filling me with blessed relief. It was a feeling I cannot explain, and I believe one can only understand this type of relief if they have also lived with the ups and downs of loving someone with mental illness. I had spent thirty-seven years desperately trying to communicate with someone who did not always want to reciprocate, so hearing from him after so long was a huge deal for me.

I felt joyful to hear my brother's happiness as he made another pilgrimage to a music festival to hear the music. He was never concerned with food or lodging; he would just follow the music. I was more than happy to send him money, so he could stay and hear the music. He was worried about the concert, and I was worried about keeping him off the streets. It had been an excruciating separation, but I never gave up on trying to communicate with Nathaniel. I do not think he had given up on me either. I had no idea, nor would I have cared in that first moment of hearing my brother's voice, that our five year reunion call would be the catalyst for the book, the movie, and a host of other opportunities which Nathaniel would only get because of Hollywood publicity and the support of a journalist named Steve Lopez. That call and Steve paved the way for an emotional reunion with my brother.

    My friend, Kim, and I first met Steve Lopez six months later in the restaurant of the L.A. hotel where we were staying. It was October of 2005, and I was nervous as we chatted with Steve. He warned me about Skid Row, before he drove us to see my brother. No warning could have prepared me for what I saw when we parked in front of a building with "LAMP" plastered across the front. There seemed to be thousands of people lying in the street. I tried to process what I was seeing when I locked eyes with a man standing on the other side of a large gate. It was Nathaniel. I could barely contain my excitement. I wanted to jump out of the car and run to grab my brother, but I was frozen in my seat; time seemed to stand still.

    The chaos of Skid Row buzzed around us, but I only saw Nathaniel. I finally ran to hug him and the first thing he said was, "You look just like Mama." I had never cried so hard and I know I will never forget that moment. Kim stood behind us crying as well. I am forever grateful to her for supplying much needed support during my brother's and my reunion in such a treacherous place as Skid Row. Steve looked on in amazement. He had never seen my brother so emotional. It was a monumental moment in my life, and I am sure it was for Nathaniel, also. The time we spent together on that trip was life changing and will be forever engraved in my heart. I was overjoyed to see my brother. He lived in an extremely dangerous part of town but was living in an apartment. Even though I saw some improvement in him, he was still extremely sick at that time, so I felt slightly comforted seeing him around people.

    Steve had found my brother when he needed help the most, and Nathaniel has come a long way because of Steve and his family. Nathaniel speaks highly of Alison, Steve's lovely wife, who has been every bit as supportive of Nathaniel and Steve in their journey to an unlikely friendship. He appreciates her immensely and feels blessed she has graciously invited him into their home and hearts. The Lopez family continues to find time for Nathaniel despite having very full, busy lives. Steve has had so many chances to give up on my brother, but he has never quit. He continues to visit Nathaniel and keeps me informed of my brother's life. It is not always easy, yet Steve does what friends do for one another. He makes sacrifices and supports Nathaniel. Most importantly, Steve is the embodiment of Nathaniel's and my Mom's hopeful dream; he has taken the time to truly get to know and befriend Nathaniel the way our mother did Ms. Powell.

    Though Steve may not have set out to stoke the fire in the mental health movement, that is exactly what he has done, and I could not be more grateful. Steve Lopez was looking for a story when he found my brother and ended up finding a lifelong friend. That is a story no one could have scripted. Steve's friendship with Nathaniel is still a source of hope for many. Of course, the hope restored in Nathaniel is clear to me most of all. Steve's articles and book have helped many people with mental health conditions, besides my brother, become more willing to speak out which you will read about in this book's chapter titled "The Letters." And of course, Steve's book brought their journey of hope to the big screen by way of the movie, *The Soloist*.

Steve Lopez and his lovely wife, Alison

The filming of the movie, *The Soloist*, was a blessing for our family in many ways. I was happy to be able to visit Nathaniel more and see his sense of pride at feeling respected for the first time since getting sick. He loved posing for photographs with people and giving out autographs. Feeling respected was the pinnacle of the movie hype for Nathaniel. Amidst the movie making hustle and bustle, a producer claimed "we are a family," yet some other people tried to keep us grounded, in their minds, by reminding me that the "fifteen minutes of fame" would end as quickly as it began. I did not think of the hype that way. Instead, I thought of how happy our mother would have been had she been alive to see the respect her son was finally receiving and how beautifully he managed it.

    Nathaniel needed blindfolding as he sat through the premiere showing of *The Soloist* movie, since the visual stimuli of a movie was too much. He was able to tolerate only listening to the music about his life. But now, he wants to write the musical score for the "next film." He had decided they should call the next movie, "A Diamond in the Rough" which, unbeknownst to him, were the same words Mom had used to describe Ms. Powell all those years ago. He insisted he would also write some of the script. Steve even bought a laptop for Nathaniel on which to write the story.

    Nathaniel's interest in writing waned with the technology, of course, so he continued with writing on the streets, walls, and whatever else he could find. I realize there may never be another movie, but that does not matter. His progress, because of hope and support, is what excites me!

Nathaniel won awards, received invitations to conferences, and even went to the White House to meet President Obama and one of his favorite artists, Patti Labelle, which I will discuss more in this book's chapter titled, "Where Do We Go from Here?" These experiences were the highlights of my brother's life. I am eternally grateful for the way the movie and Steve's book opened doors for people to have honest discussions about mental illness and for the help my brother received. The whole experience encouraged me to be bold in speaking out as a mental health advocate and for that, I am thankful.

The cameras are gone now and so are those naysayers and that producer who claimed we were family – a claim I had desperately wanted to believe. But more than 10 years after the release of the movie, people still appreciate Nathaniel for sharing his life and reach out to inquire about his well-being. For that, I am grateful.

It would take two years after my reunion with Nathaniel at LAMP for filming to begin. I realized the people working on the movie were more accommodating of us than they normally would have been. The movie staff kept me in the loop until after the movie release when my access tapered off. Up until then, they allowed me to speak with them whenever I wanted, for the most part. Jerry and I got the opportunity to visit the L.A. movie set during the filming of *The Soloist* in January 2008. They sent a driver to chauffeur us to a downtown parking lot.

The lot was full of cars, equipment trucks and other apparatus. "How much of this belongs to the movie crew for *The Soloist*?" I asked the driver. "It all does," she replied. I felt a lump form in my throat as Jerry looked at me and said, "This is big."

They took us to a vacant apartment building, first, where they were filming a scene about Nathaniel while he was living in New York. After a short tour, they suggested we leave while they filmed that emotionally difficult scene. Production told us that Jamie Foxx, who played my brother, was not comfortable with us watching him portray the psychotic break Nathaniel had while living in that New York apartment. The entire set and the preparations going into that scene felt eerie to Jerry and me. We were more than happy to leave so they could film the scene.

Next, the driver took us to LAX airport for another scene the crew was setting up. I was in awe that they had closed an entire section of LAX to film a scene, which ended up on the cutting room floor during the editing process. We realized the apartment scene had not taken long to film when they announced Jamie Foxx would be arriving at the airport, shortly.

We were walking into the airport terminal when I heard someone shout, "That's the real Jennifer Ayers!" I was dumbfounded, and Jerry remarked, "You're a star!"

I responded, bashfully, "Don't say that."

"Look at what's happening!" he marveled as I was trying to wrap my head around it all.

Robert Downey, Jr. who played Steve Lopez came to shake my hand and said, "It is so nice to meet the real Jennifer Ayers."

"No. It is a pleasure to meet you," I replied as he hugged me and smiled.

I saw Downey again later that day, but I chose not to bother him. He seemed to be in character, leaning against a trailer, and smoking a cigarette. The next time I saw Robert Downey, Jr. was at the premiere. He did not speak to us, which was okay, because so many things were happening, and I was trying to stay focused. My head was spinning by the time the actor who played my character, LisaGay Hamilton, walked over to hug me.

I had not known they were going to portray me in the movie until after it was already set in motion. They initially characterized me in the movie as an ungrateful person. LisaGay could not believe I was the person they were characterizing me as and wanted to take time to get to know me a bit. She was genuinely kind and knew the initial characterization of me was not true after spending some time with me. They were preparing to film the scene in the movie where I flew to Los Angeles to see my brother for the first time in five years and held off filming at LisaGay's request. I am grateful for her concern, because they made some changes in my character after our meeting.

LisaGay made me feel more comfortable about the situation we found ourselves in. The respect and concern she gave me eased my nerves and made me feel more confident about following her advice, which said that asking questions was okay.

LisaGay and Justin Martin's (who portrayed young Nathaniel) family believed in me and my vision for using the publicity from the movie to advocate for the Nathaniel Anthony Ayers Foundation while it was still in the preliminary stages of development. I knew I could call on them for help and they would help, as they were able, including making appearances to support the foundation. They seemed to understand what I was trying to do with the foundation and were so helpful.

I still feel like I can depend on LisaGay and feel overwhelmed with gratitude for her continued support. I feel like LisaGay helped give me a voice in the movie, because they ended up changing another thing per my suggestion after I had met Jamie Foxx – the portrayal of Nathaniel's teeth.

A member of the film production team told Jerry and I to wait outside of Jamie Foxx's trailer if we wanted to meet him. Someone told me that Foxx was "nervous" to meet me – a family member – while he was "in character," since portraying my brother was so intimate and personal for him. We waited for quite a while before he came out. Foxx did appear to be bashful around me when we met, but he was also nice.

The first thing I noticed was how badly they made his teeth look. I did not appreciate that detail, because my brother is quirky about carrying a plastic bag around which holds his toothbrush, toothpaste, and a bottle of water so he can brush his teeth, literally anywhere, when he gets the notion. My brother lived as cleanly as possible for the kind of life he was leading. The producer improved that detail after I asked.

Jamie asked me about Nathaniel's dating life and any girlfriends Nathaniel may have had. I told him plenty of girls liked my brother back in the day, but Darla was the one that stuck out in my mind. (You can read more about Darla and the girls in Nathaniel's life in this book's Appendix B titled "The Girls.") Then Jamie said, "Darla," with the voice inflections and body language he used to portray my brother. Seeing how well he captured my brother freaked me out and sent chills down my spine. It made me appreciate his acting talent, but I felt so uncomfortable I had to ask him to stop.

Jamie's kindness was even more clear when he later invited us to a celebration gathering after the L.A. movie premiere. We felt honored they included us. I did not expect to have access to any of the stars, and I made a point not to bother them either. After all, these events were commonplace for them, and we wanted to be respectful guests. The actors were kind and supportive, so much so that Jamie Foxx sent me a personal text to personally wish us a Happy Thanksgiving.

Our interactions with Jamie Foxx made me feel a little bit more comfortable asking his assistant for help with questions I had had about movie premiere details. I had assumed her expertise would help me delicately navigate the situation of ensuring my family could attend the premiere to support my brother for his big moment. When I asked her about it, she seemed surprised and sternly responded, "Aren't they going to send for your family?"

She chose to call Paramount about our situation, I believe, because she knew they should have been planning for our family to attend the premiere. I am fairly sure she told the producers about our phone call and their response was that I was "bothering the stars." That shocked me considering it was the exact opposite of what I was trying to do. The only thing I was guilty of was being ignorant of understanding the legalese and movie industry jargon in the contract they had me sign when the process began.

Eventually, I had an Atlanta attorney read our contract and he said, "They didn't really care about your brother or you." The "bothering the stars" situation was the culmination of many little scenarios that had piled up throughout the movie making process.

The first such scenario I can recall happened after about two months of my traveling back and forth from Atlanta to Los Angeles to serve as a consultant for the movie. As the day concluded and I headed back to my hotel, courtesy of the movie production budget, a movie staffer said to me, "Did you get your per diem for today?" I did not want to seem surprised and tip my hand to the fact I was unaware I should have been getting a per diem, so I briefly responded, "Oh! No." Evidently, my contract stated

I was to receive a per diem, but the language was complicated, I did not understand, and no one checked to see if I was receiving all the financial assistance due me as a movie consultant. Though those trips were a blessing because they gave me the chance to see my brother, per diems would have been nice in the beginning.

Another frustrating, ongoing scenario was the situation of our complimentary hotel rooms. Too many times in the beginning of the process, we would arrive at the hotel and either our room had not been reserved, or a credit card had not been left on file. Jerry and I, not wanting to rock the boat, placed our own credit card on file a couple of times until we learned that was not how it worked. After that, we would call the movie producers and wait in the lobby until they had straightened out our hotel issues. Foxx's assistant, the Atlanta attorney, and the movie staffer were not the only ones to point out how our care was lacking. Other Hollywood stars told us, too.

Jerry and I were sitting behind a famous Hollywood star one flight to Los Angeles. I did not want to bother him and his friend mid-flight, so I decided to hold off on saying anything to him until I later saw him at baggage claim.

I said, "Hi. How are you?"

He grumbled, "Good."

Filming for the movie was just beginning, so in my excitement I told him, "We are here because filming for *The Soloist* is beginning, and Jamie Foxx is playing the role of my brother."

He said, "Oh. I heard something about that."

The actor noticed us waiting to catch a shuttle for a rental car. With a raised eyebrow and sending me a clear message, he knowingly remarked, "They should be sending you a car."

In hindsight, I realize the movie folks were fully aware of how little I understood about the movie making process and they took advantage. I behaved passively during the entire, adventurous process, because it was a bit scary for me. My brother was making great strides, and I did not want to mess it up for him. The revelation of our treatment hurt me, but I did not complain to the movie folks. Though they did not always treat us with great care, they changed Nathaniel's life with the experience, and he did not care at all about the details. He became a "rock star" of hope to many in the public, especially to others experiencing their own mental health battles.

People still ask about Nathaniel to this day, and I learned that God had his hands on the process the entire time. At the time, I had felt like I was failing my brother, but my heavenly Father revealed to me through prayer, "We know that all things work together for good to those who love God, to those who are called according to His purpose," Romans 8:28. That helped me focus on what I could impact, like my brother and his ever changing mind.

Regardless of the logistical challenges I faced behind the scenes as the movie was being filmed, I still appreciate all that was done for my brother, including the way the producers helped accommodate us at the premiere.

Nathaniel enjoyed meeting people, shaking hands and hearing people say, "It's so nice to meet you, Mr. Ayers."

Nathaniel first said he was *not* going to attend the premiere but changed his mind at the last minute. Literally. At the very last minute, we were shuffling everything around to make room for him. We did not care though, because he was the one who needed to be there; it was his moment. When we thought he was not going to come, we wanted him represented at the premier. I called a producer and told him our idea to wear fatigue jackets since that was Nathaniel's regular attire. He was kind enough to have a courier bring the jackets to our hotel only a few hours before the premiere.

Nathaniel had also chosen to bring a guest with him who was entirely out of control. Fortunately, Nathaniel's and my sister, Del, and my dear friend and colleague, Dr. Lattimore, helped reel in Nathaniel's friend from causing a huge problem with her behavior. Yet, I am grateful to his friend for getting Nathaniel to the premiere. She was ecstatic to attend and her influence affected Nathaniel's decision to attend. Nathaniel and I were extremely happy to have shared this experience with Jerry, too.

Jerry made our Hollywood season with Nathaniel so much fun and everyone in L.A. loved Jerry – especially Nathaniel. Their respect for each other had grown as they got to know each other over the years and Jerry realized how intelligent Nathaniel really was. Nathaniel would look up at 6' 5" Jerry and say, "Man! I hope I can get to be that tall." Nathaniel looked forward to seeing his brother in law who he loved very much. Jerry died September 8, 2011.

My heart broke thinking of telling Nathaniel Jerry died. Steve told him. In fact, after 2005, Steve had the dreaded job of telling Nathaniel unwelcomed news. Nathaniel never handled loss well. It took him a long time to accept Jerry was gone. He would call and leave messages on my voicemail listing everyone, including Jerry, and asking how they were doing. He did ask me once, "How are you doing since the big guy is, you know, not here?" I told him I missed Jerry a lot.

I tried to say more about it, but he changed the subject. As time went on, Nathaniel would reminisce about Jerry, until one day when he stopped asking about him. He did the same thing when Mom died. He refused to talk about her until one day, out of the blue, he said, "The hardest thing I've ever gone through was Mama not being here, leaving." I knew losing Mom was difficult but was surprised by his comment. I thought living with schizophrenia for over 40 years would have been the most challenging thing.

Ups and Downs

I wanted to be able to stay in contact with Nathaniel more easily, so I bought a cell phone for him in May of 2009. It took him a while to feel slightly comfortable with it, but I do not think he ever enjoyed the phone. Nathaniel called me from that phone for the first time on September 11, 2009. It was the night before I delivered my keynote speech for the University of Pennsylvania's Community Health Internship Program called "Bridging the Gaps." Jerry and I were in our hotel room after enjoying dinner with my friend, Dr. Lucy Tuton, and a few of her colleagues. I could not sleep hoping I was going to deliver a message my audience would want to hear, so I sat up in bed to go over my notes. The clock said exactly midnight when my cell phone rang.

It was Nathaniel calling me for the first time from his cell phone. Undoubtedly, he had precisely planned the time. He was surprised I greeted him by name when I answered the phone, obviously unaware yet of how to program contacts on the phone. He still has no interest in catching up to technology. He asked how I was doing. I told him I was great, but surprised he was finally using the cell phone I had gotten him four months prior. Then my brother made a statement which filled my heart with joy. "I never thought I would be in my own apartment, using a cell phone," he remarked. A simple thing I took for granted was a big step to him and he was grateful. I was exhausted and struggled to stay awake as I listened to broken segments of the goings on in his life until it hit me; at that moment, I knew where he was and that he was safe. The challenge of hanging in there for that phone call vanished, and nothing else mattered.

  Nathaniel called a lot after that but never mastered the three-hour time difference between Eastern Standard and Pacific Times. He wound up getting frustrated with the phone, first, because he did not know how to retrieve voicemails and second, the worry which came from thinking he would miss a call if he forgot his phone at home. He decided he did not want to deal with the phone anymore, so I began receiving calls from his apartment's management office or pay phones. I asked about the phone. He would either tell me it was charging or not holding a charge. Calls from Nathaniel's cell phone tapered down to nothing after about 8 months of struggle. I kept paying the bill, so he would still have access to it if he needed it.

  In January of 2010, Jerry and I went to L.A. to host Nathaniel's annual birthday party. We rented Montrose Bowl and invited his friends, fans, and members of the local shelters to bowl. Nathaniel would play instruments and talk to people, if he was in a good mood, but he never bowled. He enjoyed the people, noise, respect, food, and freedom, which came with these parties. I could see my brother was sad the party was nearly over and tried hard to engage the few remaining people in hopes they would stay a bit longer. "Last call" for his party was clearly a huge struggle for him and he looked like he wanted to cry. I asked him if he was okay and, of course, he said "yes." I told him I would call him later. He said, "Oh yeah? How are you going to do that?" I said, "I'll call you on your cell phone." He replied, "I threw that thing away a long time ago." I was shocked and upset he had thrown the phone away, so I was glad he had a ride home that night. It gave me a chance to cool off before I said something I would have regretted.

  We had an early flight out, so I did not get to see Nathaniel the next day. I can laugh now as I think about how he solved the unwanted stress of a cell phone. I imagine many wish they were bold enough to toss their cell phones. He later told me it was dangerous to carry the phone on Skid Row and made him a target. He said he would leave the phone home, wonder if someone had called him, then walk home to see who might have called. He said it distracted him, which made him less safe, so he threw the phone in the trash can.

  Nathaniel's street savvy made me proud and confirmed what I had always said, "He is the most courageous man I know." He has never asked about another cell phone, but I am willing to get him another one in the future if he changes his mind. In fact, I have moments where I wish he would ask for another cell phone. I want to talk to my brother more often, even though I feel so helpless when I speak with him sometimes.

  My brother has moments of despondency, and I find myself wondering if the constant battle in his head has exhausted him. I know I would be exhausted. Seemingly innocent situations set him off easily. For example, I remember answering my work phone one day and knowing, at once, that something was wrong with Nathaniel. I have always tried to have a positive influence on him before he begins speaking, hoping positivity will infect him. Despite my desperate attempts to remain upbeat, he started in, irritated about the new case manager who had come to see him. No one told him he had gotten a new case manager. He was caught off guard, understandably upset, and certainly was not in the mood to listen to me as I tried to reassure him that everything would be okay.

  Nathaniel's illness prohibits him from trusting new people or situations easily, so of course, my brother was suspicious about this man even though he was undoubtedly who he claimed to be. Nathaniel took offense to the way his new caseworker spoke to him. His voice was raised in agitation as he exclaimed with expletives, "He's getting all in my face trying to pull rank smelling like &%$# cigarette smoke! How's he gonna come tell me what to do smelling like &%$# smoke? I thought I'd call you to see if you knew what that was about."

I always try to answer the phone when my brother calls, because I never want to miss a chance to say hello; but I was not prepared for this type of conversation. I have learned that I can interject and calm him down in some instances, but that was not one of those times. It was a situation he needed to work through at his own pace. This phone call stressed me out, because I had no idea how he might have behaved in his aggravated state. Most of the time, prayer has been the only way of helping my brother or helping me.

At that moment, I prayed Nathaniel would process the change in a healthy, quick manner, so he could move past it. I have experienced many scary, worrisome ups and downs with my brother. I had to learn that communicating with my brother would always be on his terms and would always require a great deal of understanding on my part and that of others dealing with him. The stress of learning to understand and communicate with my brother, along with fear of the unknown and concern for his well-being and even his life, has wreaked havoc on my health at times throughout my life. One such time was his birthday in January of 2013.

The Nathaniel Anthony Ayers Foundation and Able ARTS Work in Long Beach, CA (formerly known as Arts & Services for Disabled, Inc. in Hawthorne, CA) were hosting a birthday event for my brother called "JAM

Session with Nathaniel Ayers, *The Soloist*" on February 2nd at the Cultural Education Center for the Arts in Hawthorne, CA. Helen Dolas, Founder and CEO of Able ARTS Work, invited Nathaniel's LAMP friends; Dr. Ron Borczon, Director of Music Therapy, California State University; Music Therapy Students from UC – Northridge; and others who had become friends of Ayers.

I had flown from Atlanta to Los Angeles several days early to help plan and prepare for the event. My flight had lasted four and a half grueling hours. I was not feeling well at all and wound up at an Urgent Care not long after I landed which delayed my ability to see my brother. I rested little though because there was no time to waste preparing for the event. So, I forced myself out of bed and stayed on task helping with the JAM Session preparations. Though I did not feel well and was incredibly busy, I desperately wanted to see my brother.

It has always been difficult to live so far away from Nathaniel but being in his proximity has never been a guarantee he will see me. I had tried for several days to see Nathaniel without success. On his birthday, January 31, I went to his apartment and knocked on the door. I could hear him playing the violin and knew he could hear me knocking. I told him I wanted to quickly say hello. He stopped playing, so I waited to see if he would let me in. He did not open the door nor acknowledge my presence. I told him through the door I was in town staying with the Kelley's. I explained that they had prepared a delicious birthday dinner for him and we wanted to celebrate his birthday with him. Without a word, he started playing again. I went back to the Kelley's, alone. Clearly, he was not in the mood for company that night, not even mine.

Dr. Ron Borczon, Helen Dolas, and me with my swollen eye.

I did not see Nathaniel until the day of the music therapy JAM Session. I was not sure he would attend. I planned for our half-sister, Lydia, and her husband, Vance, to bring him to the JAM session, and they graciously agreed. I thought there would be a better chance of him attending if they picked him up. I waited a moment for him to process the situation after he walked through the door of the venue. I learned it was best to allow him a moment to survey a scene before rushing him into conversation. Once

I saw it dawn on him that he had come to play music, I walked over to him and said "Hello." He responded, "Hi," then went to set up his musical equipment.

Nathaniel's birthday cake for the "JAM Session with Nathaniel Ayers, *The Soloist.*"

After he finished setting up, he came over and looked me in the face for the first time since my arrival days before. He noticed my swollen eye and said, "What's wrong with you? What's wrong with that eye?" I said, "I don't really know, but I'll be okay," He said, "Yes. You have to do something about that." Then he reached over and gave me a hug. His embrace made my entire, uncomfortable, somewhat scary, and exhausting trip worthwhile.

Helen and I in front of beautiful artwork created by students in arts programming at Able ARTS.

      The event was a huge success. And the music of the JAM session had set a lighthearted, happy tone within Nathaniel; in essence, *the music set him free.* I am still thankful God pulled me through to see him have some freedom before I traveled back to Atlanta.

      My friend, Dr. Barbara Lattimore, had been my traveling companion to Los Angeles. Barbara's husband, Eugene, picked us up from the Atlanta airport upon our return home. It was late and we were exhausted, but they refused to take me home. They could see I was terribly sick and took me directly to the hospital. Eugene and Barbara stayed with me for hours waiting for the hospital to check me in. We discovered I had a severe infection in my eye, which was the cause of my swelling and tremendous pain. Later, I was told it was "Bell's Palsy," though no one ever seemed sure. I later had paralysis on the left side of my face and my right eye did not open until late May.

 I am grateful for how the Lattimore family cares for me. Barbara and her family in Atlanta and the Kelley's in L.A. have been by my side for a considerable amount of my journey with my brother. Their love for Nathaniel and me is obvious. I could not have endured nor accomplished what I have without them. I thank God for them.

 I learned upon my return from L.A. that while I was there, Nathaniel had said some unkind things to a lady and her daughter who lived near him. I heard the things he had said, and I cannot say I blame them for feeling threatened. I would add, though, that he had probably felt threatened too, possibly by the voices in his head, which is why he said such things. Steve told me later he had seen Nathaniel appearing to threaten someone in the street, which was Nathaniel's defense mechanism; start it first before someone starts something with him. That was what he was familiar with. It was then I knew something had to be done for Nathaniel's own good and safety. My brother could be a danger to himself, mainly because people not used to him could easily misinterpret and misunderstand his behavior and intentions, which all too often leads to fear and a mutual lashing out.

I did not want a misunderstanding to lead to Nathaniel becoming a negative headline in the news. I thought he needed hospitalization, as much as I never liked to admit it. I have never wanted anyone to get hurt because of my brother's reaction to the voices he may be hearing or his defense mechanism. I am also acutely aware people can be afraid of my brother when he is hearing the voices and their mutual reactions can be dangerous for one or both. I realize more than ever that the hospital stays have helped keep my brother safe during the moments when he most needed help.

 A court decided that Nathaniel had to move to a locked-down facility, because of the incident with the lady he frightened. That meant he was not free to come and go as he wanted. Some people may see this as harsh, but it was good for him at that time, I assure you. It has always been difficult to see my brother on lock-down, but I have learned to find solace in 24-hour care. His social worker told me the court was forcing him to take medication during that visit, too, which usually helps him to function better, no matter how much he hates it. Our half-sister, Lydia, and her husband, Vance, went to visit Nathaniel at the hospital. Though he refused to see them, she found the hospital to be clean with a pleasant staff, which meant so much to me. Their visit reaffirmed that this hospital stay was the best thing for Nathaniel at the time, which made me feel slightly happy. I hope and pray that Nathaniel one day sees medication and this kind of help as the Godsend it is.

    I called the hospital to check on Nathaniel. He would not come to the phone the first day. The next day he answered with a cheerful, "Hello!" I asked him how he was doing then I heard a click, and the phone went dead. I am an easy target of blame for his troubles. He was the same way with our mother when she was alive, but I know he does not believe his illness nor situation is our fault. They say people tend to hurt the ones they love the most. I later learned he was speaking exclusively to Steve at that time. Moments like that hurt, but I have gotten better at not taking them personally.

    Nathaniel's life has gotten harder as he has gotten older and his mental health brings about new challenges. Schizophrenia has continued to rear its ugly head. He lived for almost seven years in a LAMP apartment before he had to move into a hotel for a few weeks then into his own apartment. We paid rent to an agency who owned his apartment, so he had remained in good standing the whole time. He ended up getting evicted, though, because of irresponsibility often associated with his mental illness. First of all, Nathaniel wrote on the walls just like he did when he lived with mom. Nathaniel's habit of writing and hanging things on his walls and doors have proven to be extremely offensive to some people. Even knowing my brother as well as I do, I took exception to some of the things he had hung in his apartment and on the door. Then the incident with the woman and her daughter was the final straw.

The management staff at his apartment building had spoken to Nathaniel several times about cleaning his walls and doors, but my understanding was that they did not approach him consistently about it, since it related to his mental health. I know better than anyone how difficult it can be to confront Nathaniel about his behavior. Most people try to avoid confrontation, especially if they do not deal, one-on-one, with someone like my brother on a regular basis. I cannot say for sure since I live so far away, but my gut tells me the management staff did what they knew to do to make sure Nathaniel understood the consequences of disobeying their rules. Unfortunately, I think they became weary when their attempts at communication failed.

The saga with Nathaniel's apartment was stressful for me and maybe even more so for him. I would receive calls from the agency stating my brother was going to be evicted then I would receive begging calls from Nathaniel, "Please help me! They're trying to put me out!" The anxiety I felt in the situation was almost more than I could bear because I knew he was not being cooperative which always made things worse. "Nathaniel," I said, desperately trying to calm him down. "There's not much I can do from here, but I will make some phone calls." I would ask him to follow the apartment rules, and he would yell, "What rules? What rules? I don't know about any rules!" That turmoil lasted from February until he moved out on May 15, 2013, after Steve Lopez and Mollie Lowery were able to convince him to go.

    Nathaniel reluctantly packed his bags and Steve was kind enough to find him a storage space for his belongings. There was no apartment available for him at that moment, so he had to move into a hotel, temporarily. The change of environment helped him realize his new situation was healthier. He admitted to Steve it was not until he moved out that he realized the terrible condition of his old apartment. It was a huge step for him to get up the nerve to stop fighting the system and leave the mess behind. I imagine the feeling he got in that temporary hotel room felt kind of like all those times he returned to Mom's basement to find it repaired, repainted, and ready for his fresh start. I pray he always knows there are those of us who love him, want the best for him, and will never give up on him, just like Mom never gave up on him. Maybe that realization will make future hurdles seem smaller.

    Unfortunately, Nathaniel's vagabond lifestyle has always made it a challenge, at best, and sometimes impossible to keep up with him. I have not always known where he is nor how he is doing, unless someone calls to inform me, as was the situation once with his case manager, Anthony. Nathaniel had not been in the mood to talk, but asked Anthony to call me and inform me of what was happening. Evidently, my brother had gone to the emergency room for stomach pain, which had become so bad, he could not keep food down. My brother had never liked going to the doctor, so I knew he felt terrible. By the time I was able to speak with Nathaniel, he had been in the hospital for several days with food poisoning and sounded anxious. I understood the feeling, being that I was too far away to help him with anything other than a phone call. As always, I encouraged him to call me anytime he wanted.

A couple of days later, he felt well enough to talk when I called, but he did not recognize my voice right away. "Hi Nathaniel, how are you?"

"Yeah, Hi."

"You sound so much better!"

"Yeah, I do. Oh, Jennifer, it's you! I thought you might have been 'Lisa (DeLisa is a friend of mine). I did not recognize your voice at all this time. It is so nice to hear your voice though! It's you!"

We both laughed. My laugh had come from hearing in his bubbly voice that he was feeling better and well enough to laugh at himself.

"How is your weather there," he asked, "I wanted to hear about your weather more than anything in the world!"

"Really?" I asked, then went on to tell him about the snow and cold, knowing his weather was much different in California.

"Does it get as bad as Cleveland there?" he asked.

"Oh my, no way! We have had some tough winters, but nothing quite like a Cleveland winter! Two years ago, we had a terrible snow and ice storm that shut Atlanta down and a lot of people got caught out in an unbelievably dire situation for hours – even my friend's pregnant daughter. Thank God, she was able to get help! This year we got just maybe one inch of snow where I am that only lasted for a morning. It warmed up to forty degrees by the afternoon. So far, that is our winter story." He was so ready to talk. I missed chatting with my brother and was more than willing to help the conversation along.

"Have you heard any wild stories about the winter rains here in California where you are?"

"No, I haven't heard any wild rain stories." I replied.

"Well this is an extraordinary place, the way it looks," he chuckled, "It's like Colorado. Yes, it reminds me of Colorado. This must be stemming from Colorado, but I don't think any of the foothills are capped in snow."

He went on to talk about how he used to love walking in Colorado, as far as his feet would carry him! He told me he did the same thing in Los Angeles. He did not mention Cleveland where his walking escapades started. He described the view he had of the housing division across the road and the foothills beyond the homes. He was watching the planes make their way across the sky on his way to Colonel Sanders in Villa Sinai.

"Isn't that the name of that poison? Cyanide?"

"Well, there is a poison with that name," I answered. The cyanide comment clued me in to the apprehension he was feeling about being in the hospital. Schizophrenic paranoia made everyone a suspect for causing his poor health.

"Yeah well. They just ran a story about cyanide poison on my neighbor's television and I was leaning back looking over at it upside down like some kind of crazy squirrel," he chuckled. "In this interview, the lady said that she accidentally drank some of it and the nurse said what she drank was enough to kill two hundred people. She was rushed to the hospital just like me. It was very educational and really useful information to know."

Getting some music supplies.

He jumped from that to, "Well, Alysa called and, as usual, we didn't communicate too well together. Mr. Lopez was by with Mollie. You know Mollie, don't you? Of course, you know Mollie! Well, Mollie was with Anthony and Mr. Witbeck!"

As usual, I had wondered where the conversation was going. I have always liked to be able to respond in a way that will keep him engaged, but I have also learned to be patient and listen for a bit of dialogue I can grab onto to

A couple taking engagement photographs asked Nathaniel to play in the background of their celebration.

keep him talking. My strategy does not always work, but it keeps me actively listening to him. Nathaniel's hospital stays gave him moments of stability which created opportunities for visitors. This stay also brought visits from my friend, DeLisa; Professor Janise who brought sheet music to Nathaniel; Bobby, our childhood friend from Churchill who had moved to L.A.; and his friend, Adam, for whom he played the bass.

    I have moments where I look at my brother's life and wonder which of us is in a better place now. My brother has a hard life, but he does not have the same worries as other people his age – people like me. He has no need to be concerned about rent, a mortgage, car payments, or gas. He does not have to keep up with bills, credit cards, issues with neighbors, or hundreds of other trivial things that sometimes make up my day or the days of many others. My brother's main concern in life is music. When is he going to play next? Where will he play? Most importantly, what will he play? For so long, he refused an apartment because he knew the responsibility that came with that life. We were desperately trying to get him off the streets, but living on the streets created a simpler, albeit more dangerous, life for him to focus solely on his music. A life where he could play whatever instruments were available to him, no matter the condition, whenever he wanted to play.

    Looking back at the ups and downs of my brother's and my life, together, I realize Nathaniel was always trying to move forward with his life, while I was always trying to get back the person I had known before he got sick. My desire to change my brother clouded my ability to understand him. The confused, wounded, little girl in me longed for her happy, handsome, big brother who had walked into her second-grade class and attracted adoration from her classmates and teacher. If I close my eyes, I can see him smiling and winking at me as my teacher says, "This is Nathaniel class. You should all want to be like Nathaniel." Feelings of immense pride welled up inside of me at that moment as I thought, "That's my brother!" My childlike heart's desire was for my big brother to be proud of me, too. All of that got lost in the shadow of mental illness, but Nathaniel was not lost; I was.

Nathaniel's mental health was yet another thing in my life I could not control. My parent's divorce had broken our family. My dad had abandoned me for a new family. I twice had to adapt to functioning in a new family. My husband had died, leaving me behind as a widow. My heartaches and frustration with how my life had gone etched deep feelings of loneliness and hopelessness on my soul creating an incessant need to control anything and everything – especially Nathaniel's mental health situation. I had felt such a variety of emotions, including embarrassment, in the early years of my brother's illness that I stopped trying to understand him, and my need to control convinced me that helping my brother meant changing him.

I freely admit now that I had been terribly selfish, and I am sorry. Like me, he was doing the best he could trying to live his life the only way he knew how after enduring the same childhood traumas I had. I cried out to God who helped me grow, process my disappointments, mature, and finally grasp the truth that the only person any of us can ever change is ourselves. Eventually, I came to terms with the fact that my brother had a mental illness, and I could not change nor control it. God helped me realize that my brother and I were survivors, and with His help, we could make it through anything.

Visiting my big brother Nathaniel.

". . .life is a blank canvas, or a blank musical score, and we can do with that canvas or score whatever we choose."

A Trip Home

I attended my first high school reunion 40 years after graduating from John Hay High School. That trip to Cleveland was different from most other visits, because I wanted to see people I had not seen in years rather than visiting for a loved one's funeral. I had not planned to talk about Nathaniel, but it was unavoidable since many of my classmates remembered him from the news, the movie, and/or his walks through the streets of Cleveland. Apparently, his story, our family's story, touched lives, especially a high school friend of mine named Archie, who had graduated a year ahead of me.

Archie was a handsome, high school track star who made us laugh with his great personality. Archie and I were sitting at a table with some other friends when he said, "Did y'all see her on 60 Minutes?"

Archie was surprised that some of my classmates had not seen my interview and bragged on me saying, "What? She represented us well!" I was surprised by his excitement.

"How is your brother?" Archie asked as my classmates listened intently.

"He is doing much better now, after being forced to move. He could not really understand why that was happening to him. But it seems he is in a much better situation, and the people who are collaborating with him seemed to be interested in him."

Archie went on to explain how proud he was to be acquainted with Nathaniel and how "awesome it is that he is from John Hay High School." His enthusiasm and willingness to sit down, look me in the eyes, and express his pride and concern for Nathaniel truly touched me.

Another friend named Michele sat down, clearly showing the same strength she had always carried while we were in school, which greatly affected me then and was also impacting me at that moment. I am positive she did not know how encouraging her strength had always been. She was an includer who would not allow feelings of insecurity or worry to prohibit me nor any of our other friends from picking ourselves up and choosing enjoyment and fun in life. While I never did share too much about my brother growing up, opting to bottle things up, I felt Michele was one of the few people who I could have talked to, if I had chosen to, and she would have never judged Nathaniel nor our family.

My trip down memory lane had begun, though, when Greg, my cousin, greeted me at the airport. Greg and I were always close through the years. He was someone on whom I could depend even though he had fun harmlessly flirting with all my female friends. He always helped me in every way he could. Greg was a Cleveland firefighter and would stop now and then to ask Nathaniel how he was doing if he saw my brother walking the streets. Of course, Greg knew he would not always get a clear answer, but stopped, nevertheless. The drive through town on our way to Aunt Willa's brought back many memories, and I was ready to get the journey through memory lane started. My cousin, Debbie, was also at Aunt Willa's when we arrived. I welcomed her warm greeting and all the hugs. Later that day, we went to visit a Senior Center for Aunt Willa.

Admittedly, Aunt Willa wanted to find somewhere with activities to keep her busy and out of her house. Our round-trip ride to visit the first center took us by East 95th street where my life had begun. We decided to stop by my childhood home, and my heart raced in anticipation as my mind filled with vivid, beautiful memories of my childhood before my world had drastically changed.

All my joy and memories melted away within ten seconds of seeing my childhood home, though, as I realized time and perspective were thieves. A small, dilapidated, empty house with a small "for sale" sign on the door had replaced the large home full of love the child in me remembered. The wrap-around front porch and wide, inviting steps we used to congregate on were missing. The large backyard where Nathaniel and I used to play with our dogs and each other was overgrown and someone had cut down the apple tree. Why did it seem so small?

I was only a little, innocent girl when my family had lived in that house. I suppose everything seems bigger and brighter when we view the world through the lens of a child. Perhaps it seemed smaller because my family was missing. They say it is family that makes a house a home. Perhaps it seemed smaller because the happier times I had known before were gone. Before my father left. Before my brother's diagnosis. Before marriages and divorces and deaths. And Hollywood.

Debbie and I got back into the car with Aunt Willa and headed down the one-way street as my mother did every day to head to Flo's Beauty Lounge, though we did not have to go back the wrong way, like she did. I saw the apartment building where I had jumped from the second story trying to catch up with Nathaniel. Mom's beauty shop was a shell of a building and the apartment building was boarded up. I seemed to be drawing attention from the residents as I began to take pictures of my old neighborhood. I explained to one woman that my family had lived just down the street about 50 years ago, and I remembered my brother playing football in the street. Her tension with my presence seemed to ease just a bit.

A car pulled up with two young men who abruptly demanded to know if I was coming to tear down the apartment building, insisting it "needed to go." I told them no and explained to them, too, how I used to live on that street. They laughed as I told them the story of jumping from the second story of the apartment building chasing after my brother. It was then that they began to see me as one of them instead of an outsider. I asked if they had ever heard of a movie called *The Soloist*.

The driver said, "Yeah, I heard of that movie with Jamie Foxx who played this who dude had some problems."

I smiled and said, "Yes. That guy was my brother and we all lived on this street."

"No kidding," one of the men said. "It wasn't like this then, was it?" he asked.

I said, "No, it wasn't. I just came into town for my high school reunion, and I have been wanting to get by here for the longest time."

"What high school?" one of the men asked.

"John Hay," I replied.

"What reunion is this for you?" they asked.

"It's my fortieth!" I said with pride.

One of the men yelled out, "What?!" I did not know if it was a good or bad "what," but I chose to believe he thought I looked too young for it to be my fortieth high school reunion.

"Where's your brother now?" one asked.

"He is in LA," I replied.

"Where do you live now?" another enquired.

"I am in Atlanta."

"Oh, The ATL!" We all smiled. The men told me to have an enjoyable time at the reunion and welcomed me "home."

"Thank you. And yes, this is home." Any threat they had perceived by my presence, or mine of theirs, fell away as they were able to see the love coming from my heart. It was clear to me that they were looking out for the neighborhood. It was a very deep moment which allowed me to momentarily remember my old neighborhood for what it used to be.

So much had changed since I called this place home, though, and it had nothing to do with the size of the house, nor the missing porch, nor the missing apple tree, nor the hollow beauty shop. I had changed. The little girl who had lived there had not experienced the world the way I had. She did not dream much, because that street had held her entire world. I, on the other hand, had learned to see the truth of life and learned to hope and dream, because of my brother.

I learned to bravely face and endure my journey, no matter how enormous the trials seemed. I learned that taking life's journey, one step at a time, forces the trials to become small enough to overcome. I had also learned there will always be another huge house with a wraparound porch, apple tree, and a big backyard, and the mature perspective I had gained, sharpened by life, would help me recognize it. Despite the maturity of my new, grown-up perspective, that visit has remained a challenge because of the contention that lingers in my mind between the perspectives of little-girl and grown-up me. My trip down memory lane continued the Saturday of my trip when a dear, longtime friend of 30 years came by to see me. Bruce and I had not seen each other in years. He agreed to take me to see my siblings' and my Alma Mater,

John Hay High School, after mentioning I was longing to roam the beautiful halls again.

    Bruce and I noticed students gathered outside of the school that Saturday morning. They told us they were there for help with the SAT. They said we had to go through security to get into the school. A security guard greeted us as we entered the school. I told him I had not been back to John Hay High School since graduating in 1973. He exclaimed, "Whoa! Then this is way different for you!" The kind gentleman went on to explain the school had three different programs, a new gym partially financed by Charles Oakley, and kids now had to apply for admission to attend John Hay High School. It gave me chills to hear how prestigious John Hay High School had become. I told the security guard I was in town for my class reunion and asked if I could look around. He gave us permission to tour the school and my friend, Bruce, was as excited as I was, especially since he was an educator.

    I reminisced as we walked the halls and could almost see myself, 40 years prior, passing my classmates in the hallways. I noticed things I did not pay attention to as a young student; the building was a gorgeous display of craftsmanship and the most beautiful architecture – a true work of art. I was simply in awe. You could tell the school took immense pride in what they had by the excellent condition they kept everything in right down to the shiny floors. I found myself reflecting on the history made while my siblings were in school there. The Cleveland Riots made history, but neither of my siblings ever talked about it. Nathaniel, instead, chose to focus on his music and his beloved string bass.

The beautiful halls of John Hay High School

Remembering Nathaniel's time at John Hay prompted me to set out to find the band room. They no longer had a performing arts program, which made me sad. I could only imagine how sad Nathaniel would have been to know the arts, including music, were gone. I headed for the auditorium where Nathaniel had acted in "Porgy and Bess" and "A Raisin in the Sun." Bruce and I found an open door that led us into the dark, balcony level. Looking down, I could not believe how enormous that auditorium was. I was amazed that my brother had stood on that stage and remembered all his lines in front of a full house. His memory was a gift. He had acted and played instruments in front of hundreds. Mom and I had attended each one of my brother's performances at John Hay High

School. Her smile had lit up the room as she beamed with pride for her "Tony." We never missed going backstage, so Mom could hug my brother and tell him how well he had done. Nathaniel's opportunity to perform in that auditorium was a pivotal time in his life with his music and acting. I also remembered standing on that same stage with my friends Ernestine, Marvin, Robert, and Carl for a school talent show singing "One Less Bell to Answer." We had called ourselves "The Portraits." My emotional strength began failing, and I found it difficult to stand in that auditorium with my memories. I told Bruce, "I've seen enough." I was happy to have had the opportunity to see my school, but sad thinking about all that happened there many years ago.

    I wondered how my brother, a sentimental man, would feel walking the halls of John Hay, and what kind of memories would surface. I know he had good and tough times at John Hay, although I never knew all the details. I remember hearing him telling Mom about an incident that happened at school one day. Our mother shook her head saying, "No, No, No…" not wanting to hear more about it. I never asked what it was about, but I know the conversation ended abruptly, and Nathaniel seemed unsatisfied by our mom's reaction.

    John Hay High School inducted my brother into their Hall of Fame in 2010. It was an honor they recognized his outstanding talent while attending John Hay High School. Our sister, Del, accepted the award on

Nathaniel's behalf and gave a short speech. A friend and fellow football player, John Hicks, was inducted into the Hall of Fame at the same time as Nathaniel. John and I had discussed organizing a fundraiser, a few years before he died, for the Nathaniel Anthony Ayers Foundation. He admitted to me he could not watch *The Soloist*. He said he did not want to see his old teammate and friend in that frame of mind. "I want to remember the guy I played ball with as he was back then: handsome, smart, and talented."

  Bruce and I had to drive by the old Fairhill Mental Hospital when we left John Hay High School. It had been converted to a facility for the elderly. I asked Bruce to pull over, because I was trying to find a halfway house named "Hillhouse" near Fairhill that someone had told me about. Jon, a former Social Worker at Fairhill Mental Hospital, had told me Hillhouse was a separate facility. He had said my brother was a resident there for a while. Bruce and I discovered it was across the street from Fairhill. I vaguely remembered a rehabilitation facility also being on site at one point.

  Jon was 29 and my brother was 28 in 1979 when Nathaniel was a resident at Fairhill Mental Hospital. Jon said he did not know much about my brother's musical background until one day when they were walking across the grounds together. Jon said, "Nathaniel started talking about music. He began to talk about the classical composers he liked, and he told me his favorite piece was by Bach. He began to hum the piece which totally caught me off guard. I began to realize what a talent Nathaniel was. I felt like a picker in comparison to him once I heard him play. Nathaniel would always say something profound, but sometimes, he can be hard to follow. Once I thought about it, I would think, 'How did he do that?' Or 'How did he produce that?' He was always making remarks which I refer to as 'spiritual,' because they were so cerebral and thought provoking. I have always had such warm memories of Nathaniel. And no, he did not like to take medicine then either. But I did not want to force him or come across like I was scolding him." Jon and Nathaniel often bonded over music and eventually realized they both had studied under Harry Barnoff - someone they both highly revered and respected because of his mentorship and the classical music education he provided to them.

Mr. Harry Barnoff, now over 90 years old, was my brother's music teacher at the Cleveland Music Settlement when Nathaniel was a young teen. He had also been a member of the Cleveland Orchestra and the U.S. Army Field Band. Nathaniel still has so much respect for Mr. Barnoff, so I try to connect them, by phone, as often as I can. When my brother has a chance to talk with Mr. Barnoff on the phone, Nathaniel recites music tidbits he learned from Mr. Barnoff decades prior. Hearing that my brother never forgot what he was taught, Mr. Barnoff got emotional during one phone call and said, "Nathaniel! You remember that? I can't believe you remember that!" It is touching to hear. A short conversation with Mr. Barnoff can always turn Nathaniel's sour moods to positive ones.

Jon once told me he always admired Nathaniel's talent and was honored to have been in his presence. He lamented, "I would love to see him and Harry Barnoff together again." Jon also told me that after reading *The Soloist: A Lost Dream, An Unlikely Friendship, and the Redemptive Power of Music* and seeing the movie, he was somewhat disheartened because that was not the Nathaniel he remembered. I explained to him the pain of judgment Nathaniel had had to endure since Jon had known him, and that my brother had learned to adapt, as best he could, to a society which did not understand nor cared to understand him or his health challenges.

Jon went on to share about a brawl, which had taken place at Hillhouse while my brother lived there. Apparently, Nathaniel did not take part, but it had such an impact on the residents that they kept pieces of a banister that had broken during the incident and presented them to Jon as an award at a facility awards ceremony.

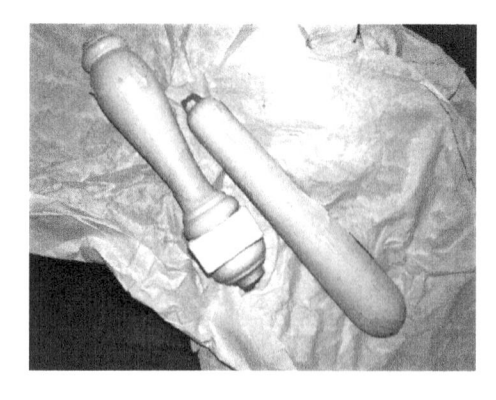

A Piece of the Banister

Jon kept those pieces for years and later mailed a piece of the banister to me as a keepsake. I stared at the grounds of what used to be the Fairhill Mental Hospital and the Hillhouse halfway house and imagined my brother and Jon strolling the grounds talking about music. For a moment, I felt at peace until I remembered the abrupt change toward mental healthcare which happened during the Reagan administration and caused places like Fairhill Mental Hospital to suddenly close. After that happened, too many mentally ill patients who still needed to be in treatments were wandering the streets without the help they desperately needed to keep them, and others, safe and healthy.

I was at work one day when such a man wandered into our building. That man and people like him could apply for general relief or some type of public aid in our building. That man was clearly not ready for that kind of autonomy. He was big, strong, and burst through our door with seemingly superhuman strength, like the Hulk. Security tried to detain him which set his mind in defensive mode. It was frightening watching nearly all the security guards in our building try to detain him for our safety. The man had hurt several of those guards. I assume he wound up in jail, since they had just closed Fairhill Mental Hospital at the government's direction.

That incident stirred up more worry in me about my brother. The mentally ill already had to face an exhaustive list of challenges in life without situations like this increasing fear in the minds of the public. Masses of people who live in fear of situations or people they do not understand can be dangerous, especially when sensationalized news stories like incidents with this man stoke their fear. This man's experience made me afraid for Nathaniel. I was terrified he would become a target. That evening I began doing what I could do; I prayed for that man, for my brother, and for all those displaced with no idea where to go.

Bruce was quiet, knowing I was deep in thought and overcome, once again, with emotion. I said to Bruce, "This is heavy, and I can ONLY imagine the agony my brother has gone through, throughout his life with this illness." I just shook my head and said, "I'm ready to go. Thank you for bringing me here." Bruce, uncertain of how I was feeling upon leaving the old Fairhill Mental Hospital, decided to treat me to a tour full of fun, amazing history, and a delicious lunch at Yours Truly. I had needed the distraction but could not shake my haunting thoughts of Fairhill. I was grateful to have been with Bruce at that moment. He allowed me to be vulnerable, sharing my innermost thoughts, and he gave me intelligent, thoughtful feedback.

I believe with all my heart that it is important to look back on where you came from and find the positive side. Romans 8:28 says, "And we know that all things work together for good to them that love God, to them who are called according to his purpose." I do know that God takes whatever is meant to harm us and uses it for good, so I have learned to take all my memories of hurt and pain and have chosen to see love, laughter, and hope intertwined through it all. I know God has a plan for my life, although I do not yet know where I am going.

    My childhood home was a huge house to a little girl who did not dream much, and because of my brother, I learned to hope, dream, and see life for the truth of what it really is. And of course, later in life our mother had to learn to dream because of her son. I have learned that you must live through every journey and trial. When it is right there in front of you it can be enormous, but as you grow, the journey begins to become the right size and small enough for you to conquer and overcome. But there will always be another huge house, with a wraparound porch, an apple tree, and a big backyard. Using this analogy makes it easier for me to keep going and to see every situation for what it is. If the situation I am in is bad, then I try to see it for what it could be, positively and conquerable, through my new, mature lenses. I use these lenses when my brother calls me, and my new perspective helps us to laugh, reminisce, talk about my lack of musical knowledge, and even disagree on sports. Maybe he will ask me about golf one day. I imagine that conversation would keep me on my toes.

"I finally decided, after years of heartache and losing myself, to take a step back and come to terms with the fact that I can only control me and my actions."

Losing Our Father

I received a text message at 12:59 pm EST on June 17, 2014 saying, "Dad is not doing well today, so we are going to see him and will let you know how he is." At 2:05 p.m., I responded with, "WOW! So much going on. So sorry to hear that!" At 10:47 pm, "Dad just passed."

My first concern was for Nathaniel upon hearing of our father's death. He does not like to discuss death and struggles, terribly and openly, when he learns one of our loved ones has died. Since Steve is always the one with the daunting task of telling my brother the news from our family, including deaths, I emailed him explaining what had happened. Once again, Nathaniel refused to acknowledge the news Steve told him about our father's death, but at least we had made the effort to ensure he knew. I, on the other hand, did not know how to feel about the death of my father, considering we had never been close since he left us when I was a small child.

I grappled with the decision of whether I should attend the funeral. I found myself entertaining every possible excuse: the cost; the time off work; rampant thoughts like, "He wouldn't care. He didn't come to my mother's home going," making myself believe he did not care about me nor my siblings. I grew disappointed with myself for being so conflicted. I sought serious counsel and prayer after which things started to fall in place. I found a great price on an airline ticket and a place to stay with my friends, the Kelley's, who had become like family. They said, "Don't worry about anything," and they meant it! Lisa even offered to go to my father's going home service with me. I could not have asked for a better support system. Yet with all the blessings coming my way, I was still finding reasons not to go – weak, invalid reasons.

One of my weak reasons was a potential bladder infection. I was at work one evening when I barely made it to the restroom in time, because of the sudden onset of an overwhelming pressure on my bladder. I overreacted and told my co-worker, "Well, that's it! I have a bladder infection. I can't fly." Her descriptive facial expression told me I was being ridiculous as she said, "Just sit near the restroom." She was right, of course, even though she had no idea of the internal struggle I was going through. I was fine, as it turned out.

Next, I made the date of the service an issue. I received a text on Thursday, June 19, 2014 from my half-sister, Lydia, saying, "Hi Jennifer, dad's service will be on Monday, June 30, at 3:00 p.m., Forest Lawn Mortuary in Hollywood Hills."

I responded with, "I'll do my best to see if I can find a reasonable ticket."

"Ok," Lydia responded.

It dawned on me that the service was to be on a Monday, "With the service being so soon, there is no way I can get a reasonably priced ticket. Today is Thursday!"

"I guess just keep trying every day and hopefully you can find one," Lydia responded.

I lashed out, "Well, it seems as though there was no consideration made for people (his children) who don't live in LA, but I'm not going to worry about it. If it had been a little later in the week, I would have had a better chance. Moving forward, I at least hope our names, as his children, will be in the program/obituary. It would have been nice if someone would have CALLED, at least, to see if Monday would have been convenient for me living in Atlanta and Del living in Cleveland. No worries, though. All is well."

She set me straight, "That is one of the reasons why we are having it on the 30th. We did consider everyone out of town!"

The 30th! I pulled up her text, and there it was. The combative thoughts in my own mind, warring with themselves on whether to go to the service, had created a haze which blinded me from seeing the truth: I was out of excuses. It was no one's fault but my own. I had more than enough time to book a flight, and I needed to go. I apologized to Lydia for flipping out. She would have had no idea that my real struggle in getting to L.A. had nothing to do with planning. My healing, but still broken, heart was the culprit. Everything fell into place for me to make my way to L.A. Somewhere inside I thought, or maybe willed, something would go wrong preventing me from getting to L.A. It did not.

The Kelley's met me at LAX with open arms. After lunch, we stopped to visit Kelvin Kelley's father in the nursing home. He was terribly ill yet thriving during our visit. I wondered if my father had received such diligent care. I had only visited my father that one time in the nursing home, which set my brother's healing back months. The Kelley's visit with their father in the nursing home was radically different from my visit with my father. I was happy for them but felt a bit broken-hearted for myself. My mind wandered to the callousness of my father's words and behavior, and I thought perhaps my father's behavior was because of the illness he had fought. That thought snapped me back to reality and helped me put things in perspective. I was in LA. with my dear friends visiting their ailing dad while waiting to attend my own father's funeral.

The Kelley's had done their absolute best to make my visit to L.A. an enjoyable one, despite the fact I was there for my father's funeral, and trying to visit with Nathaniel was not always easy – especially when he was in emotional turmoil like he was over the death of our father. The Kelley's know I love golf, so they took me by Trump National Golf Course (before his presidency), which is an incredibly beautiful, public course. I had to laugh, looking out over the course, remembering the story of Steve taking my brother to a driving range to hit golf balls. Nathaniel thought, as do many first timers, hitting the ball would be easy. I have personally witnessed the story Steve told me about Nathaniel's experience. My brother took a whack at the ball with such force that he spun himself around and missed the ball. I understand he got better. I was so impressed with the course and staff, I promised myself I would go back and play it and bring Nathaniel with me to hit some golf balls together. Unfortunately, I have never made good on my promise to myself.

    The Kelley's knew how much effort I put into making my visits wonderful experiences for Nathaniel, and how drained I became in attempting to prepare for all possible outcomes of trying to connect with my brother. They knew I had traveled many times to see Nathaniel only to be unable to find him. Other times, he would make me wait if I was 15 minutes early, or I would have to deal with his sour attitude for the duration of my visit if I was 5 minutes late. I did not want to see him, on this visit, prior to attending our father's going home service. I did not want any problems this time or to upset him in any way. He hates to talk about death more than anything. I wanted to have as pleasant and easy of a visit as possible, especially since the thought of not going to the service had crept into my mind again.

    The morning of the service, I was feeling a little anxious until I answered an unfamiliar phone number, which came across the screen of my cell phone at 10:33 am.

"Hi Jenny. How are you?"

"Nathaniel!" I shouted.

"Yes, it's me."

"Oh my God. I'm so happy you called me!" I said.

"Yeah, I was just thinking I should call you. Where are you?" he asked, knowing I was in L.A.

"I was going to surprise you, but I'm in LA. I will be there to see you in the morning. Do you need anything?"

"Well you shouldn't have to come all the way to LA to get me anything. It will just be good to see you, BUT a burger would be nice." We both laughed.

"It's so nice to hear your voice," he spoke in a way I had not heard in a long time. He sounded well. In my mind, I imagined the undertones of his comment to mean, "It is so good to talk to you and hear your voice without my illness overruling our interaction."

I responded rationally and genuinely, however, with, "It's so nice to hear your voice, as well." I am always happy to hear from him, but it was especially nice under the circumstances.

"You sound great! I am SO happy to hear from you!" I got emotional and the tears began to fall. He could hear it.

"You're going to make me cry," he said as he also started crying, "I'm going to do better and call you more."

"I'd like that, and I am going to find a way to get out here more often!" I responded.

I thought about confirming that he understood our father had died, but I just could not do it with how well our conversation was going. Death of a loved one seems difficult for Nathaniel to accept. Our mom's death was the worst for Nathaniel, taking him years to acknowledge, because she was the person whom he loved more than anyone else on the face of the earth. He cut Steve off, refusing to hear anything about our father dying and has never spoken to me about it. It seems he just does not know how to deal with death; or maybe I do not.

The phone conversation with my brother that morning was wonderful and entirely lucid. It made me feel lightheaded and giddy. It was a conversation I had dreamt about for many years. I started jumping up and down and praising God after we hung up. The song, "HAPPY," transformed into a gospel worship song for me at that moment and did flip, flops in my mind. My friend, 'Lisa, joined me in my joyful hand raising and praising. I had to force my focus back to the fast-approaching home going service of our father.

I was edgy because I was unsure of what to expect. Hardly anyone at my father's service knew who I was except Lydia, Sarah, and my stepsisters, and why would they? I recalled that painful blow in Atlanta when my father shocked his friend by revealing he had children other than those in California. He never spoke of us, so it felt we did not exist to his family outside of Cleveland. I was in agony wondering how they would list my siblings and I in the obituary or if they would list us at all. DeLisa and I continued to the church once we received directions from a guard on how to navigate the huge cemetery. DeLisa and I prayed before entering the service, which eased my discomfort only a little.

When I finally met up with Lydia, she was truly kind and wanted to introduce me to her family. She gave me the choice of meeting them before or after the service, but I decided the sooner the better. Fortunately, we arrived early which allowed me the opportunity to meet most of them. We walked down the narrow aisle of the little church to reach the people she wanted to introduce me to. One of my father's stepdaughters exclaimed, "I never thought I'd see you again!" I had thought the same thing.

The service was nicely done, but I felt uncomfortable listening to the first minister talk about all the good things our father & his wife did to help others. I realized I did not know the man they were describing. That man was not my father. The pastor acknowledged there were three children from my father's previous marriage, but he did not mention our names. Each minister spoke about the ways my father and his wife had inspired them. I realized then that my half-sisters, Lydia, and Sarah, had no idea how Del, Nathaniel, nor I felt about our father. Biologically, we had the same father, but an entirely different man and dad had raised them.

They played a video presentation of my father's California family life during the service. They had plenty of good memories with their dad, but there was not one picture of me nor my sister in the presentation. Nathaniel did make it in the video, though. No one asked me if I had any pictures I wanted in the video, even though I had only one photo of Del, Nathaniel, Father, and me I would like to have shared. The obituary was very generic, offered no details of family, and the service went ahead as if my father was still married to his wife. It was better that way, protecting them from needing to elaborate on the tragic details of his two divorces and abandonment of his first three children.

    The video made me hurt even more, driving home the fact that me and my siblings never got the chance to be a part of our father's life. He was not there for us, emotionally or financially, and only rarely visited which caused problems with his wife back in California, or so he said. For some reason, his wife could not tolerate him visiting nor communicating with me or my sister. My father had told me his wife's harsh demands in the divorce papers she served to my house were because of his visit to me. At 80 years old, my father was still blaming someone else – me, this time – for his marriage falling apart. I imagine the divorce was just as hard on my half-sisters as it was for me all those years ago.

    It took me well into adulthood, emotional breakdowns, and lots of prayer to allow God's grace to work in me to the point where I learned how to communicate with my father. I have always felt badly for

Nathaniel who never seemed to know how to reach our father. Our father never tried to understand my brother when they did connect. Our father was in denial of Nathaniel's illness until the day he died, and he hurt my brother on more than one occasion saying, "You can do better if you try!" Our father hurt Nathaniel for most of his life. I have often wondered how much of my brother's emotional instability and sensitivity stems from our father's careless relationship with him. As for my sister, Del, she said she had one extremely terrible experience with our father many years before which ceased her efforts to reach out to him ever again.

    The whole, awkward day was challenging for me knowing I was in a place where I clearly did not belong. Despite feeling odd, I continued to be my genuine self. I could see my half-sisters – especially Lydia – were trying to help me feel more comfortable, and I am grateful to them for that. I am also eternally grateful to my friend, DeLisa, for attending the service to support me. I certainly needed it. As for my father and the relationship between his wife, Nathaniel, Del, me and him, I pray that God in Heaven has finally given him and his wife peace and rest.

Where Do We Go from Here?

I had small thoughts as a child. I lived within myself much of the time, internalizing everything, and did not think too far ahead or too far beyond my surroundings. Nothing mattered to me other than what existed within the small circle of my family. Everything and everyone I needed was right there. I managed myself the same way when my brother first began to show obvious signs of being ill. It was huge to me. I did not have the words to express how I felt, so I did what came naturally to me; I watched everything and internalized it.

As my brother's illness became more profound, I buried myself in a web of my private thoughts, feelings, and judgments all skewed by the deceptive lenses of an innocent, confused, hurting child. After mental illness manifested in my brother, I do not ever remember hoping for anything more than for him to be well again. I hoped for the youthful, undaunted fun we used to have. I desperately wanted life to be like it was in our childhood home. I wanted only those memories to be my reality and wanted to make more just like them. I wanted him to be the same Nathaniel as from East 95th Street. But the harsh reality was that we could never go back, and I buried myself deeper in my web which has taken years to try and unwind.

As time has progressed, experiences like my 2013 return to my childhood home on East 95th Street in Cleveland have continued to give me hard reality checks. The huge house I remembered from my youth is now just a rundown shack that holds many memories, but its days are numbered. The enormous wrap around porch, which accommodated my playtime activities, is gone, and I now realize it could never have held hundreds of kids like my child mind had thought. The apple tree is now lifeless, and our manicured backyard is now nothing more than a plot of weeds. I now understand that memories of places and events in my past seem to morph into new realities once I get to view them through more mature lenses of time and perspective. This revelation helps me better understand the natural progression of life and my analysis of it.

I personally know how challenging it is to extend yourself to help a person with a mental illness, especially one who is close to your heart like a parent, child, sibling, or spouse. It took years of me trying too hard and making too many mistakes to stop projecting and spinning my web around Nathaniel trying to mold him into who I wanted him to be. I finally decided, after years of heartache and losing myself, to take a step back and come to terms with the fact that I can only control me and my actions.

One thing I passionately believe now, after taking that first step back, is that I must take care of myself, first and foremost. It is like listening to the flight attendant's instructions on a plane, "You must make sure your own oxygen mask is in place, before you help the person next to you." It does not matter if that person is your child, spouse, parent, or sibling. You may not survive to help another if you do not first take care of yourself. I can only help Nathaniel if I am doing okay. It has been hard to do and has taken me years to leave that old home in my heart and walk through the door of the new place in my heart, which is so much more. The truth is, I still find myself swatting away strands of judgment and deception, remnants from my childhood, I push to stay focused on what is huge now.

The way mental illness affects our country and how few people are talking about it is my huge reality now. I am thankful more people are willing to talk about mental illness than they used to, but the stigma continues, and the fact remains; not enough healthy, positive discussion is happening. A cookie-cutter approach will not help every individual, but it is my dream for us to work toward a better future where more people become educated and less fearful of the mentally ill.

I have met some outstanding people, because of Nathaniel, who are trying to change societal views on mental health. Some previously not brave enough to speak out are now advocating, with force, through public speaking, blogging, authoring books, and advocating for others to be more open and share their experiences. The journey we face as siblings, caregivers, parents, wives, husbands, and relatives of a person with a mental health condition is fraught with challenges society sweeps under the rug until something tragic happens like a school shooting or suicide. When tragedy strikes, mental illness is the hot topic for a brief time before collective amnesia sets in again about the importance of staying the course with the mental health community.

    My hope is for positive instead of derogatory dialogue to be default when referencing those diagnosed with a mental health condition. Not every individual needs to work hands-on with the mentally ill, even though the mental health community needs these types of volunteers. But support can happen in other ways like being intentional about stopping snap judgments and donating to organizations who support the mentally ill and their unique talents. That is what I appreciate about The National Alliance on Mental Illness (NAMI) and the work I had done with them, which ended because of COVID-19. They have knowledge of resources and programs, and they work with other local and national agencies, which I have had the pleasure of interacting with when giving presentations. I have had a great deal of success referring people to The National Alliance on Mental Illness for help.

    Once my perspective shifted and I came to terms with what I *could do*, I decided to start helping Nathaniel at a grassroots level by raising awareness amongst family and friends. I began a blog at www.HearTheMusicWeb.blog

and started posting updates on Facebook to let our friends know what was going on with Nathaniel. I am also doing a podcast entitled "Hear the Music. A Conversation With" where I talk with people who have similar experiences or who are willing to share their unique story. The love and support from our Facebook friends made me feel much better. Nathaniel is not remotely interested in learning about Facebook, but I do pass along the sentiment in the posts when I can. He always smiles, wants to know more, and asks me to "tell everyone hello and thank you."

 A great multitude of people care about Nathaniel and what is going on with him. I want everyone who is battling mental health conditions to receive the same support my brother does. I am not sure Nathaniel is always aware of all the people who appreciate and care for him. I know he has had moments where he realized how appreciated he was though, when we have attended events like The National Alliance on Mental Illness and the American Music Therapy Association conferences. At the NAMI conference, they celebrated him by allowing him to play nearly all night. He did not play perfectly, but he played passionately. I wondered what was running through his mind that night which stirred him to actual tears. His teary-eyed performance touched the audience; the proof was in the line that formed around him asking for an autograph or photo. Nathaniel was elated and accommodating.

He got the same reaction at the American Music Therapy Association conference. He was an attraction and an award recipient, though the focus of that evening was different. AMTA was emphasizing the importance of supplying music therapy for groups. But when Nathaniel began to perform at the AMTA event, the event took on a whole new meaning. Organic, authentic jam sessions began springing up as other musicians wanted the chance to play with my brother. Once again, he stayed up all night jamming with anyone who wanted to play with him. Other musicians began to scatter as the night wore on, but Nathaniel continued to play the piano and cello at the same time, by himself, which I posted on YouTube. It was amazing. My brother, *The Soloist*, verified his namesake, and he was outstanding.

Steve invited Nathaniel to play at a book signing in LA in 2010.

The movie, *The Soloist,* did well, and in the wake of its release, more people than ever were talking about the issues surrounding mental illness. But my brother sacrificed something in that process, which was especially important to him and the only thing he really had in his life: his privacy. He had opened his heart and his life up to the world, and that brought him joy and laughter as well as pain and a multitude of other emotions he had suppressed for a long time. He allowed himself to be vulnerable, and I had hoped during that time, more than ever, that his vulnerability would raise awareness for the mental health community allowing him and everyone else who were alone, misunderstood, or suffering to get the full support they deserve.

We knew the best time to get steam behind our mission was when the movie buzz piqued across the nation. Unfortunately, it seemed that a few people in his inner circle were only interested in going to Hollywood to walk the red carpet. After the movie premiered, there were those who did not understand we had genuinely been trying to get help for my brother and other people like him. I even remember hearing someone who served in our foundation say, "You've had your 15 minutes of fame!" That hurt.

My heart ached, because it was never about the fame nor attention and our goal to make a lasting difference would never end after the hoopla died down. Clearly, our passion to help the mental health community and Nathaniel was not as important to them. I decided to let go of their harsh words and sentiment over something they did not understand, and I forgave them. I gave everything to God and continued to press on without them. As for Nathaniel, he is a noble man who will always be important to me and many others as is clear by how many people ask about him, regularly. One person who never abandoned Nathaniel nor questioned our mission after the movie buzz died down was Steve Lopez; he was and is the faithful friend who helped Nathaniel express what was in his heart, and in return, Nathaniel did the same for Steve and many others.

    I have learned the hard way that this is not a journey to travel alone. It is one in which you must create a support system. I have developed an excellent support system all over the country; one I had never predicted but was blessed with, nonetheless, as I stepped into my role as advocate and public speaker. I had never planned to become a public speaker, but I am thankful for that mantel which came to me, since it has given me incredible opportunities to stoke fires for advocacy and say "thank you" from me and Nathaniel to people from all walks of life; people who have dedicated their lives to serving, healing, and producing sensible, comprehensive, and effective resources in the mental health community.

    My brother has also found a support system not only in Steve Lopez, and his friends from places like LAMP, but also in his old Juilliard classmates, Joseph Russo, and Yo-Yo Ma. I am thankful for these two men because they continue to extend respect to Nathaniel. Yo-Yo Ma does not see Nathaniel often, but at one point he reconnected with my brother whenever he was in Los Angeles for a concert. The Los Angeles Philharmonic staff was gracious enough to extend an open invitation to Nathaniel to attend these concerts. I tagged along once, and Nathaniel was glad I got to go. He dozed off a little during the concert, so I nudged him to stay awake. He got a little irritated with me, but I ask you. What are little sisters for? He became more alert near the end of the concert. He must have been a fan of the piece they were playing because he began to quietly conduct from his seat.

  The L.A. Phil's publicist, Lisa White, came to escort us down to the reception for Yo-Yo after the concert. Many at the reception greeted Nathaniel with a great deal of respect. Lisa allowed Nathaniel in the small room where Yo-Yo was standing. When he saw Nathaniel, he greeted him with a handshake and a huge smile. Nathaniel said, "I remember when you came to Cleveland to play and you were just a kid." Nathaniel then listed the music his friend had performed. Yo-Yo Ma, surprised, stopped in his tracks. He seemed shocked that Nathaniel could remember that concert and the music he performed. He said, "My God, Nathaniel, you remember all that? That is amazing!" Nathaniel said, "Why wouldn't I? You are great!" Yo-Yo reached up to hug him and kissed him on the cheek. My brother introduced me, and I received a kiss on the cheek as well. Nathaniel asked Yo-Yo Ma for his autograph on his program. He obliged then said, "I should be asking for your autograph." It was such a great moment for Nathaniel, and I am glad I got to be there for it.

Joseph Russo and Nathaniel were able to reconnect after Juilliard, thanks to Steve Lopez. During my first trip to Los Angeles, Steve had taken Nathaniel, Kim, and me sightseeing in his car. My brother was getting impatient riding around, so Steve called Joseph to allow Nathaniel to speak to him. He talked about music with Joseph for about 45 minutes. None of us understood their musical discussion, but Nathaniel's laughter helped all of us. That

My brother, Nathaniel Ayers, meeting President Barack Obama at the White House

conversation with Joseph took the edge off and helped to shift my brother into a better mood.

I felt elation hearing Nathaniel communicate with an old friend who was patient with him and seemed to genuinely appreciate my brother. A few years later in 2010, the Obama Administration invited Nathaniel to the White House to play for the 20th Anniversary of the Americans with Disabilities Act. Joseph drove from Connecticut to accompany Nathaniel on the piano for his White House performance. Joseph was amazingly kind to drive from Connecticut to accompany my brother and dealt with my

President Barack Obama and me at the White House

brother's nervous behavior wonderfully, he was so accommodating and patient.

Prior to playing, Nathaniel had the pleasure of meeting President Obama. It was one of the happiest moments in my brother's life. Nathaniel managed himself, beautifully. President Obama greeted my brother by saying, "Hello, Mr. Ayers." Nathaniel replied, "President Obama. President Barack Obama. God bless your presidency, sir! The president of the United States of America. Praise the Lord!" They shook hands and looked each other straight in the eyes as President Obama said, "It is a pleasure to meet you, Mr. Ayers." I will never forget Nathaniel's beaming smile. It was clear to me that President Obama had done his homework and knew how my brother preferred to be addressed. For a while, Nathaniel had been calling Steve, "Mr. Lopez" and Steve called my brother by his first name, in return. At one point, my brother took offense to that title arrangement and had decided it would only be fitting and respectful that Steve call him "Mister" as well. I am sure my brother felt respected when the President of the United States of America called him "Mister Ayers."

Joseph and Yo-Yo are doing well and making a living from the music they love so much. They started out at the same place as Nathaniel and while I am happy for their success, I wonder what my brother's life could have been without this illness. My brother is doing better now living in an environment where he does have support and I wish him much happiness. I hope he will be able to play in an orchestra again, because he talks about that often. He talks of traveling, not taking medication, and not being ill. I believe that is his way of expressing his faith. Our mom planted a seed of faith in her dream, too, when she put to action her declaration, "I want to do for Ms. Powell like I want someone to do for Tony." It has been a blessing to see the harvest of her seeds of faith manifest in the help my brother continues to receive from Steve Lopez.

    This story will never end for me so long as God allows me to live, even when I am gone, another family will share our story. Now is the time to unite. All of us need to listen, stop judging, speak out, and pull together to help end the stigma associated with mental illness allowing those individuals and their families who are suffering to feel empowered to get help. We must shine a light on the need, the needed resources, and the available resources. We need to keep fighting for those who need us.

    I hope conversation surrounding mental health never stops and people all over the world open themselves up to "Hear the Music" like my mom and Steve Lopez. I know that too often people are like I was when I spent too many years trying to force my music on my brother, not hearing his unique and beautiful song. But the truth is, there are billions of unique songs begging to be heard.

    I finally heard my brother's song, once I stopped trying to get him to play my musical score. I also learned that just as the greatest symphonies we have ever known have multiple movements, each starkly unique in the emotions they stir, the music of our lives is the same. Instead of only four, standard movements though, the movements of our lives never stop changing. So, I must keep listening and respecting each new movement of each unique symphony, and so must you.

Los Angeles Philharmonic Orchestra principal pianist, Joann Pierce Martin, and her wonderful husband, Garvin, also an accomplished pianist. They have always been exceedingly kind to Nathaniel.

He will always find time to play.

"Stay strong and keep trying."

Hearing Others Music

Many individuals and families have emailed me over the years to share their own stories, and I have stayed in contact with many of them for the past ten years. I was truly fortunate to meet a woman by the name of Rebecca who became ill while in college. She first contacted me through The Nathaniel Anthony Ayers Foundation (now known as the Friends of Ayers Foundation) to let me know she enjoyed the movie. She said it had encouraged her to help by being more vocal and open about mental health awareness, but she was apprehensive about speaking out. Fear held her back, but I wanted her to feel safe talking to others. We shared our mutual struggles without fear of judgment and discovered common ground. I felt blessed and encouraged by her desire to learn more about my brother and our situation, as well as trust me with her challenges.

Rebecca was a published author by the age of eighteen with her book called, *Heart to Heart: A Daily Devotional for Teenage Girls*. She was one of the youngest, published authors with Thomas Nelson at the time. Her accomplishments and potential were incredible, and I wanted her to receive as much help as she could get to keep her on the successful trajectory she had already begun in her life. I mentioned to her, after our relationship had developed, that Janssen Pharmaceuticals was looking for individuals willing to share their stories. She was apprehensive, but her mother's support gave her the courage to take part. She took part in a powerful Janssen documentary called, "Living with Schizophrenia."

Soon after the documentary release, Rebecca started a blog advocating for a local center in her hometown, which serves the mentally ill. The travel and speaking engagements intensified with Janssen, and Rebecca told me she was struggling with the workload. They had wanted her to travel to New York for a screening of the documentary, but she was not sure she could handle the pressure. Experience taught me that one should never push someone with a mental illness beyond their limits, so I talked through the pros and cons of the New York trip with her.

I encouraged her to ponder whether she would regret missing the opportunity to share her story at the screening. I acknowledged it would be a wonderful experience for her but not to push to herself beyond what she thought she could handle. I also challenged her to change the way she was looking at the experience. I said, "Don't think of it as an obligation, but rather something you want to do for yourself." She decided to go and had a wonderful time. Rebecca and her mother are both strong advocates for those affected by mental illness, and I am proud of the way she continues to grow.

The first time I met the immensely talented artist, Jerome Lawrence, I was attending a panel discussion hosted by The Fulton County Office of Disability Affairs discussing disability concerns in the workplace. Jerome was there discussing his firsthand experiences of living with schizophrenia. His story and eloquent speaking skills impressed me and gave me hope. The whole panel riveted me. I was eager to introduce myself to him after the panel had concluded in hopes he could give me better insight into understanding Nathaniel.

I told Jerome that Nathaniel was a talented musician but had to drop out of Juilliard because of his mental health. I also shared my brother's schizophrenia diagnosis with him, and he gave me a look which seemed to say, "and so what?" I went on to explain that Nathaniel was not taking medication. Jerome got quiet then asked, "He's not? Does he still play?" I was not sure, because it was during one of those periods where I had not heard from Nathaniel. "I am sure that if he can play, he is," I responded. Jerome told me he had had, "a lot of support, and it was not easy." I felt awful, since I did not know where my brother was at that time. We wished each other well and went our separate ways.

Jerome and I met again a few years later. By then, many things had changed, and he had learned about *The Soloist*. I was still working at Fulton County and handled coordinating the annual food drive, which collected nonperishables for the Atlanta Community Food Bank. The County partnered with The Nathaniel Anthony Ayers Foundation (which was just developing) in this venture. The Atlanta Symphony Orchestra (ASO) joined the County and the fledgling Foundation in our efforts by allowing us to place food barrels and *The Soloist* posters outside the concert hall to ask for food donations.

Jerome had set up his incredible artwork, also. It was Jerome's artwork, which helped me understand a scene in *The Soloist* I had initially disliked. The scene tried to visually show Nathaniel's mind through a two-minute flash of psychedelic colors and sound. I had thought the movie scene was strange and pointless, but Jerome's artwork exploded with bursts of colorful paint and gave me a new appreciation for that part of the movie.

Jerome also took part in a panel discussion hosted by The Carter Center about *The Soloist*, alongside Steve Lopez. Additionally, The Nathaniel Anthony Ayers Foundation (Event Sponsors), The Atlanta Chapter of the Society for Neuroscience, The Snatcher Health Leadership Institute at Morehouse School of Medicine, and The Carter Mental Health Program held a question and answer session after the film for students, mental health professionals, and caregivers.

The event was full of knowledgeable people and valuable information, but the moment which stood out to me above all was when an audience member asked, "Why won't people who have a mental illness take their medication?" Jerome answered, "I have been dealing with schizophrenia for a long time. My doctors tried many medications, and it took an exceptionally long time to devise a medicine regiment that was good for me and that I could function with." He went on to explain how different medications made him feel and how they were not right for him. He said, "It takes a lot of effort, time, and support to produce the right combination. Not all medication works the same for everyone with a mental illness. It took almost eight years for me." That really struck a chord with me. I knew, all too well, from personal experience that there is no "one size fits all" when it comes to treating mental illness, and support is a key ingredient for success.

Nathaniel had also had the privilege of performing with Peter Marshall from the Atlanta Symphony Orchestra during the event. He did not seem to understand what was going on, though, so Nathaniel was not in the best of moods for the event. I have learned that Nathaniel feels nervous when he does not have enough information which makes him grumpy and *very* irritable. Unfortunately, that happened in the case of this event, and made it a tough day for Nathaniel. He relaxed a little once he and Peter began playing, but he did not play his best.

My brother is his own worst critic and perceives a "less than his best performance" as a failure. He struggles to let those moments go, so they can fester for days making his mood worse. I always hope, for his sake, he performs better the next time. It breaks my heart when he gets down on himself, and these moods can make it very difficult for me, or anyone else, to help him. In this instance, we were late getting to the airport the next morning for his trip back to California. I felt terribly about that, especially since I had begun getting him ready the night before. But after the emotional rollercoaster he felt from the event and his performance, he simply had not felt like leaving or going anywhere quickly.

All in all, it was a wonderful event with an at-capacity crowd. Peter Marshall was so gracious and kind with my brother. Nathaniel did great, despite what he thought, after he got through his nervous episode. But Jerome's comments had the most impact on me.

Alex W. wanted to share his story shortly after he was diagnosed with schizophrenia. Alex is a writer and comedian who uses humor to help cope with his illness. I had the privilege of meeting Alex near the beginning of his journey when he was learning how to push forward and deal with his diagnosis. I was impressed with his work he shared with me. In one email he wrote, "With schizophrenia, the voices you have to deal with are what make it so hard." Still, he found a way to joke about his problems.

Alex mainly focused on the voices he was hearing when we spoke, particularly in the beginning of his illness. I did speak with Alex on the phone, once. It was a short conversation, but he seemed glad we could talk. I was certainly honored to speak with him. Although we do not keep in touch, I search for updates on him to see how he is doing. At that time, I learned from Alex that my brother might still be hearing voices, even if he does not admit to it. I realized that much of my brother's behavior could be the result of voices he might hear. I am thankful for the short season I shared with Alex, because he helped me understand my brother a bit better.

Janssen Pharmaceuticals hosted a conference on health disparities called *Schizophrenia Awareness* and invited me to sit on a panel for the National Alliance of Black Journalists. Prior to leaving for DC, I met a young lady also from Atlanta, Ashley S., who was scheduled to be a part of the panel, too, and Janssen thought it would be good for us to first meet in Atlanta to get acquainted. Ashley's story was powerful, but what she is doing now is even more powerful. She started an organization called, "Embracing my Mind," where she shares her story and offers encouragement through group sessions. Her organization also trains police how to handle encounters with someone who may have a mental health condition.

Ashley is trying hard to educate the public on mental health. Her drive and willingness to speak candidly about her diagnosis is uplifting. She owns her story and makes NO excuses for what happened. She is active with the local National Alliance on Mental Illness (NAMI) and often gets the chance to share her story through them. She even spoke with CNN's Dr. Sanjay Gupta in 2011. Ashley is willing to present to audiences of 10 or 1,000; it does not matter. She is determined to make a difference no matter how big or small. I will always admire her, greatly.

I was grateful to have gotten the chance to speak to a packed auditorium of students at Guilford Technical Community College in Greensboro, North Carolina. The group of young people were the same age as Nathaniel when he became ill. I told them, "Don't be afraid or ashamed to get some help if you begin to feel like you need someone to talk to or like something is happening to your thoughts and your mind." Then I shared my family's story. To my surprise, there was a line of people who came up afterwards asking for a photo or autograph and wanted to share their own stories.

One young man said, "Thank you for sharing your story. You remind me of my sister. If not for her, I would not be attending college now. It is because of her that I am here. Hearing how much your family has gone through makes me appreciate her even more." His comments hit me hard and reemphasized how important it is for me to keep listening and sharing. I found his openness encouraging. We must keep working hard to help everyone "hear the music." I hope that the young man and his family are doing well.

I received an email from a lady who had been unable to leave her home because of her battle with depression. She told me her husband brought home a copy of *The Soloist* and after watching it, she felt more inspired than she had in a long time. She wanted to change her life and had set a goal of getting out of her house again. I have not heard from her since, but I hope she found her way into the open.

A young student at Stivers School of the Arts in Dayton, Ohio emailed me to talk about her time there as a violinist dealing with mental health issues. She felt separated from the other students and like she did not measure up. She told me watching *The Soloist* motivated and encouraged her. The girl's grandmother was kind enough to let me send a copy of the book and a t-shirt to her granddaughter. The Grandmother later told me how those items had raised her granddaughter's spirits, which of course, raised mine. She said her granddaughter proudly showed those items off at school. I also received a video of the talented girl playing in the orchestra. She was the principal violin, and she was awesome.

  I found another friend in Dr. Elyn Saks, a law professor at the University of Southern California. She shares her story in a powerful book she wrote called, *The Center Cannot Hold: My Journey Through Madness*. She is open about her health and still respected enough that a TV network asked for her opinion on the series, *The Promise*. They wanted to correctly portray a man with a mental illness and asked for her advice. She is a busy woman, but still tries to meet up with me when I am in Los Angeles. She offers as much support as she can to our family and has even attended Nathaniel's birthday parties.

  Dr. Saks encouraged me to author this book. She sent an email to me after reading a few pages which said, "Have read your pages and just love them. You write well and tell a compelling story. Obviously, Nathaniel's story is good and important, but yours as a loved one is too." I was so relieved and inspired. She is someone who understands my story because of her own experience. She shared some of her story with Nathaniel when she met him. She said, "I was diagnosed with schizophrenia, too." My brother got noticeably quiet. I could see the disbelief on his face since I had introduced her to him as **Doctor** Saks. I was hoping her story offered him as much encouragement as it did me.

 I mention my interactions with these people, because I think of my brother whenever I hear a story from a person who fights through a mental illness. I know if it were not for Nathaniel's mental health, he could have been successful like his old classmates from Juilliard, Joseph Russo, and Yo-Yo Ma. But he spent years on the streets in the throes of judgement and disrespect because an illness named "schizophrenia" was winning the battle with him.
 I have personally seen the disturbing stares Nathaniel receives from people in public. Those stares have always made me nervous because I never know how he will react. A while back, a television show called "What would you do?" aired an episode about a man who had fallen into difficulty and became homeless. He simply wanted to sit in a restaurant and eat a meal. It was terrible how some treated that man. Some of the restaurant patrons wanted management to ask him to leave. He was not even mentally ill. It hurt me knowing that my own brother has continued

to endure similar reactions to him. I can only imagine how tired Nathaniel is of getting laughed at, shoved, beaten up, and disrespected, sheerly because people are afraid of what they do not understand. I have not always understood my brother, either, but lack of understanding never gives one the right to be cruel.

    Admittedly, I have had moments in the past where I crumbled under the weight of judgment and tried to control Nathaniel's actions to mitigate against awkward situations because *I* did not want to be embarrassed. I tried to convince others I was trying to change the way my brother dressed, talked, and acted because it would make it easier for him in the world. But the truth was I tried to change him for me. It took a long time for me to grasp that he was okay with who he was and is, and so should I be. Nathaniel had had a difficult enough time dealing with strangers, so how dare I judge him alongside them. I learned to let go of my image of who I thought my brother should be and give him due respect for the man he is, and that means everything to him. I eventually learned he is quite a guy and everything he does has meaning. Whether others or I get it is entirely our own problem, not his.

    I have also learned that one cannot know for certain how they will manage a situation until they are directly in it. A mental illness diagnosis sends the individual and their immediate caregivers into a tailspin of emotions like shock, fear, and embarrassment. "Simply" figuring out where to go, what to do, and finding doctors and facilities who genuinely care feels like trudging through a quagmire. Almost certainly, those diagnosed, and their caregivers, will feel the nearly crushing, unfortunate weight of judgement bearing down on them from strangers, family, and friends, alike.

Nathaniel at a LAMP picnic in 2009 with the famous bra. The bra around his neck, and often around his cello, meant no harm. It was just another way he expressed his artistic talent. He is not currently using his artistic expression.

As if the challenges which follow diagnosis are not difficult enough, those who have never experienced living with nor dealing directly with those suffering from mental illness, like Nathaniel, tend to offer generic suggestions and opinions on what they believe will help the situation. *Their naivety prompts judgement and their self-appointed entitlement prompts them to spew hurtful sentiments without having walked in our shoes.*

Through the years, everyone has had an opinion about what they think we should have done to help my brother, though they were not the ones living with him. A relative once told me an in-law of his had read *The Soloist* and felt we should all be ashamed of ourselves. They believed we did not try hard enough to help Nathaniel and keep him off the streets. I was upset initially then wisdom and experience helped me to laugh at their conclusion because it is easy to *think* you know better than everyone else while looking at a situation from the outside in. I would have been more than happy to talk with that person to help them get a more in-depth understanding of our journey, but I realize it is easier to judge from the sidelines than to get in the middle of it and learn the truth about what families and caregivers go through.

I am confident we did the best we could have for Nathaniel, and I pray that person never has to experience it, firsthand. It has become easier to recognize good, but clearly ignorant, intentions. For me, those opinions have always been like listening to someone without children give advice on how to raise them. What they could never understand is that Nathaniel has always been his own man, and we could not force him to do anything he did not want to do.

Most of the time, getting help for a mentally ill loved one is a partnership, not a dictatorship. I would listen to most uninformed opinions because I knew they meant well, but it would have been nice to have had someone to talk to in those early days who had firsthand experience, like I do now. I wish I had known, then, the amazing people I mentioned earlier.

I am glad my brother has been able to share his story, because it has changed his life. I can see now how his openness with his story has helped change the lives of many others. It opened new opportunities for him and encouraged others to see him in a different light. I am grateful for the people who follow the Facebook page and ask how he is doing. Nathaniel has been difficult to keep up with since his diagnosis, because the disease seemed to gain the edge after my brother's refuge, our mom, died making it nearly impossible to keep track of him.

Schizophrenia makes it a challenge for friends and loved ones to communicate with Nathaniel in his, sometimes peculiar, way. Even worse, it causes him to completely cut off communication with us, for extended periods of time. But my connection to these beautiful people and their stories helps me feel close to my brother, even when I am not.

Nathaniel received this jersey for Black History Month. The 19 is for our Mom's birthday. He called me that day to say, "you missed a good time."

    As I write this, my head feels like it is about to explode with all I would like to share. This is my effort to help others feel free expressing themselves. I have chosen to share what has happened in my life and how my family and I saw fit to deal with our experiences, for better or worse. My willingness to be open by listening and sharing has allowed me to meet many wonderful people and learn a tremendous amount from those suffering from mental illness, their caregivers and from those who have never been closely affected by it either.

    Keeping the conversation going and growing through beautiful people like I have mentioned creates a community which helps us all as we journey through this challenging life of mental illness. I beg everyone to remember that people like my brother, are just like you with plans, hope, and dreams for their lives, despite a mental illness diagnosis. They never imagined they would wake up one morning not recognizing themselves because their own minds had betrayed them. Mental illness is indiscriminate with its victims and can manifest at any time, changing the dream trajectory of even the most intelligent, goal driven person. We need to find the strength to hold onto those dreams for them, because their lives and dreams are every bit as important as those of someone not suffering from mental illness.

These amazing people have shown me that life is a blank canvas, or a blank musical score, and we can do with that canvas or score whatever we choose. We should paint from our hearts and only paint what is uniquely ours. Our unique creation is a beautiful masterpiece whether others understand it or not. By sharing our unique masterpieces, we give others a chance to learn who we are. I have also learned that reciprocated sharing and listening creates a mutual respect which makes it easier for others to hear our own stories.

Everyone's story is unique, but much is the same. What was best for us may not be best for others, though. Some people will not find my story important or relevant to their lives, and that is okay. But I will have accomplished my goal if even one person feels a little less alone in this world after reading this book. I wish I could do more to help those going through tough times, but my words will have to suffice. My prayer is to connect across the miles with families I will never have the privilege of meeting. I hope they find hope in my story and pay it forward by reaching out to others to end the stigma surrounding mental illness.

Seeing my brother at LAMP in L.A. after a 5-year separation. Words cannot describe my joy or my relief.

Others Like Us

Several years ago, a journalist discovered Ted Williams, a homeless and admitted addict, on the streets of Columbus, Ohio. Ted was using his natural, notably talented voice for panhandling passing cars when he happened upon the local journalist. The journalist recorded Ted's considerable voice-over skills. The video went viral and so did Ted's fame. He became the Kraft Macaroni and Cheese commercial voice saying, "You know you love it." People jumped all over a seemingly good opportunity, but it was merely a good opportunity for a news story and monetary gain for some people – not Ted. The attention Ted received was nice and brought about many opportunities, but they exploited his talent before addressing his serious issues.

It seemed that Ted's mind became overwhelmed and not strong enough to manage the barrage of media and public attention. It quickly became clear he needed a lot of help. The situation reminded me of my brother, Nathaniel, and our mom, in some ways. My heart went out to Ted's mother when I saw her interviewed. It was obvious she had carried a heavy burden long before the camera showed up at her door. Her interview seemed restrained as if she did not have permission to offer much to the media. Her excitement with Ted's fame seemed tempered, taking a "we will wait and see" attitude on whether it was good or not for her son. Ted also had children who were hurting because of his serious issues. They would be adults now. Of course, the media has faded entirely, but at least the public is aware of Ted and his story. I hope and pray the attention he received paved the way for the rehabilitation he needed and help for his mother and children. I also hope someone has given him the chance to consistently work on his gift in a safe, encouraging environment.

Ronald Davis was homeless when an interview with him went viral on YouTube in 2013. He really touched my heart as he shared his pain caused, in part, because of the horrible things passersby would say to him to humiliate him. He wanted a job, a home, and food to eat, like everyone else, but he was "not presentable" which made it challenging for him to find work. His life started much like many others – in the suburbs – before he fell on tough times. Potential employers would sneer and say, "We'll give you a call," even though it was clear he did not have a phone.

Ironically, Ronald worked long, difficult hours on the street, starting at 6:00 AM when security would force him from wherever he was sleeping. He would shake a cup for change in hopes of getting enough money to sleep and eat in a shelter for one night. Ronald recalled one man who had been cruel to him returning to apologize. The man said he had had a difficult day and should not have taken it out on Ronald. The man gave him $30 and told Ronald to find a bed and food for the night. I am glad that man was convicted enough to help. It seems funny to me how people can be so mean without giving a second thought to what tomorrow could bring for their own lives. I hope someone gives Ronald the chance he deserves and pray his life improves because of his honesty and willingness to pour out his heart to a stranger. I truly hope the truth will set him free.

In the window of time it took for me to write this book to its publishing, I learned that Ronald Davis never got the chance he needed. He died, homeless and nameless, on the streets. His son did not find out his father had passed until a month later, because Ronald did not even have an identity card.

Steve Harvey once hosted a homeless man on his television show. The homeless man admitted that alcohol was the culprit in his homelessness. He said his young daughter was in foster care because of his and her mother's instability; her mom was an alcoholic too. The man, a talented sketch artist, said he wanted to make a change and hoped to get his daughter back someday. At some point, he was offered a place to stay. He said it was difficult to stay in the apartment given to him. He had no other household possessions, so the Steve Harvey show helped by giving him clothing and household items. They shared his artwork which was incredible. This man's story was familiar to me. His difficulty with staying in his apartment reminded me of the trouble Nathaniel had moving inside. He had lived with the noise and chaos of the streets for so long that the confinement and responsibility of his apartment filled him with anxiety. Nathaniel had left the faucets dripping to help soften the silence of those first, quiet nights.

    I am grateful my brother has never had an issue with addiction, like that man and too many others with or without a mental illness diagnosis. Drinking never interested him. He broke a childhood habit of smoking long ago and grew to despise it. I am not a doctor, but I have seen, firsthand, the affliction caused by substance and alcohol abuse. I have also seen mental illness declare war on the one diagnosed, their family members and caregivers. Alcoholism is classified as substance abuse – not mental illness, but everyone knows it certainly *alters* mental functionality and can lead to mental disparity. I pray this dad finds success with his artistic skill and stays sober, allowing him to regain custody of his daughter giving her a chance to break the cycle of instability and to feel the love of a supportive, successful father.

I caught the tail end of an interview one evening after watching the tragic news of the Sandy Hook shootings. They were interviewing a woman whose son had schizophrenia. She said her son had become completely detached from his family and the world he had grown up with. Days would pass without a word from him until suddenly, he would appear at her door, completely out of it and in a world of his own. She had tried for years to get help for him, to no avail.

The media did a follow-up story about that woman's son saying that Grady Hospital in Atlanta had seen the story and reached out to help her family. Her son is now on medication and doing much better. I wish I could have talked to her. I would have shared with her how my family went through the exact same thing starting forty years prior. I would have encouraged her and helped her to know she was not alone in her struggle.

It breaks my heart that things have not changed more. My conviction and determination to speak out for the mental health community is partially motivated by my broken heart. Advocacy and public awareness are the only way many mentally ill ever find help. If you are reading this, please do not give up. Stay strong and keep trying. Eventually, your loved one will respond to a treatment which works for them. I pray that day comes soon for you.

For my brother, it is music, but it took a long time for him to break out of that "homeless" mindset. He is a different man today, yet his needs are still great.

Fortunately, someone had noticed and met the needs of these individuals, in big and small ways, because they were able to Hear the Music, even if it was just for a moment. People do not need to be suffering from schizophrenia, like Nathaniel, to require help. Mental illness, substance abuse, and homelessness all take a toll on a person's physical and mental well-being, and that of their families. I hope every suffering person will be fortunate enough to find someone compassionate and bold enough to set their judgments aside long enough to hear the music of those suffering and support them in the same manner as my Mom, Steve Lopez, Steve Harvey, and the unknown man who listened to his conscience.

The Letters

Nathaniel once called to ask me about email. It made me smile when he asked how people were able to connect so quickly, and it made me realize even more how out of touch with the world he was. I tried explaining to him all the new ways we had to stay in touch; cell phones, internet, and email. I could tell he was getting frustrated, and even though he does not care to understand this technology, it does make him happy when I share with him about all the people who use these avenues to reach out and ask about him.

The impact from the release of *The Soloist* has reached far beyond Nathaniel and our family. It started a conversation about mental illness many people had never heard before, and in some cases, did not want to hear. Illness of any kind is an unpleasant topic for most people. We do not like to think about people we love being vulnerable to something like mental illness nor do we like the idea of being vulnerable ourselves. Admitting that Nathaniel was different was something my father could never come to terms with and it affected his relationship with our whole family. We need to be able to talk through the tough things, so we can move past them and help those affected live their lives to the fullest. After the release of the movie, my brother started receiving cards, letters, and emails from others who were going through the same things themselves or were walking through similar things with someone they loved. People wanted to share their stories and offer encouragement. A lot of these letters came from children. I wanted to share some of their letters here. No one is alone in this journey and if we encourage one another to speak out, we can all "Hear the Music."

To whom it may concern:

In my English class this year, I watched a video about Nathaniel Anthony. Nathaniel Anthony got me into trying to learn how to play my violin. Before I saw him play, I did not think that the homeless could change people. I never thought that the homeless could play instruments very well.

When my teacher showed me Nathaniel Anthony play, my teacher told me they made a movie of him called *The Soloist*. When he was homeless, he still knew how to play instruments. The movie soloist might inspire a lot more people. One day I would like to meet him in person.

I am writing this letter to show my support for the Nathaniel Anthony Ayers foundation. I would like to know if there are other ways to help.

Sincerely,
Victor C.

To Whom It May Concern:

In my English class this year, we read about Anthony Ayers and the challenges they had to overcome. We watched his biography, and it was very interesting. So, my mom and I went to go buy the movie, it was good. It was amazing seeing the things Mr. Lopez did for Anthony.
After seeing Anthony and Mr. Lopez's story, I was inspired. They have stuck together even through the ups and downs. Seeing how Mr. Lopez helped someone that needed help inspired me to do the same. Please accept my donation as a sign of support to Mr. Lopez and Anthony Ayers. I would like to learn more about their situation and how I can help.

Sincerely and Happy holidays,
Adam T.

Dear Ms. Moore,

On behalf of the Coalition of Mental Health Professionals, Inc, its Board of Directors, guests, and friends would like to express our gratitude for your assistance and support in having Mr. Nathaniel Anthony Ayers (Tony Ocean) perform for our 20th Anniversary celebration. Our event is entitled the Extraordinary Sunday Afternoon of Visual and Performing Arts. I must tell you, all our guests thought it was just that, EXTRAORDINARY! One of our staff videotaped his performance and I will try to send it to you. I will also email you the pictures taken by our photographer.

Please find enclosed the check for the honorarium. We hope this check will be helpful for the continuation of the Nathaniel Anthony Ayers Foundation. We are also thankful to Professor Janise White and Steve Lopez for all their help in making this event possible. We would like to invite Mr. Ayers back again next year if possible.

Warmest Regards,
Sandra C.

To Whom It May Concern:

    In my English class this year, I read and watched about Nathaniel Ayers and how he was a talented African American at Juilliard. He had a nervous breakdown and dropped out of Juilliard. Ever since then he has been homeless. He still plays instruments and I know his main instrument is the cello.

    It has been very sad and heartbreaking to see people like Nathaniel with such talent to see them on the streets without a home. I would not want to see people like Nathaniel with so much talent on the streets homeless. I am writing this letter to support the Nathaniel Anthony Ayers Foundation because people deserve another chance at life and not let their talents go to waste.

Sincerely,
Jabari H.

To whom it may concern:

    In my English class this year I read about Nathaniel Ayers and his hidden musical talent. We read Steve Lopez's article from the LA times that described how Nathaniel was found playing on the streets of Los Angeles. The article of Nathaniel led me to think about how a person with such a musical talent can be put into the disgusting shady areas of the streets. How can a person be comfortable with just a violin with two strings and say, "I have found happiness in this world," when that person is homeless? That is why it amazes me that a person can live with only their most prized possession music, the thing that can fill anyone's hopes. I would also like to thank Dr. Barbara Lattimore, Board Member, Director, Fulton County Department of Mental Health, Developmental Disabilities and Addictive Diseases for helping the NAAF to become an organization. I hope my donation will help musicians who are in situations like Nathaniel's. Please let me know of any other ways I can help.

Sincerely
Jasmine R.

To Whom It May Concern:

    I am a ninth grader and in my English class this semester we learned about a man named Nathaniel Ayers, a former musician who had a mental breakdown and is now a homeless man in New York. We learned about how a person's life can change in the blink of an eye, and how even the most unfortunate people can have talent and that people can be underestimated due to their state of being. Learning about Nathaniel Ayers touched me in a way that I felt for him.

It has been interesting to learn about this foundation, being a musician myself, I can feel for Nathaniel. When I learned about this because it touched me because I know very much about undiscovered talent. I felt angry because everybody has talents, but many are not able to express it because of their lifestyle and choice. I hope that I can help this cause in any way possible.

I am in full support of The Nathaniel Anthony Ayers Foundation, and would like to discover more about it. Please accept my donation and I would like to learn more. Thank You.

Sincerely,
Mark E.

Dear Nathaniel,

My name is Nancy K. and I live in W_____, Ohio, which is near Cleveland. I am 40 years old and I have suffered from schizoaffective disorder and obsessive-compulsive disorder since I was 13 years old. I saw a preview for the movie *The Soloist* in 2009, although I have not seen the movie yet. I do not know if you know what schizoaffective disorder or not, so I will tell you a little bit. It is a form of schizophrenia with a mood disorder (mania or depression). I have wanted to send you a letter since I saw your website on the internet and read about the Foundation for the artistically gifted.

I am interested in your story and your Foundation because I can relate to you even though I do not know you personally. I can relate to you because you have a severe mental illness as I do, and because you have a love of music and art as I do. I have a collection of 24 poems that I have written, and I have put two of them in with this letter for you to read. I have seen the things on your website about the Foundation programs two or three times, but I do not know exactly what each one of them offers. I have a lot of trouble thinking clearly because of my problems, and it is just too much for me to try and figure it out for myself.

I have different interests, but I am particularly interested in knowing if your Foundation offers programs in creative arts such as floral design, and creative writing. And second, I am interested to know if you have a program for performing arts (vocal instruction, and possibly musical instruction.) I am also possibly interested in donating a small amount of money to one or more of your programs.

I know exactly the suffering that people with mental illness go through- all the pain, suffering, and misery. Broken dreams and feeling like you have been cheated out of a happy life. I do not think I will ever be able to put into words all the torment I have felt from my problems. Sometime in the future, I want to read the book *The Soloist* because I am curious to know more about you.

A few years ago, I sent a letter to a publishing company with two of my poems for them to read. I asked them if they wanted to put those poems into a book with other people's poems and publish it. They wrote back to me (I still have the letter) and said that if they published a book with my poems it would have to be only my poems and I would have to have 30 to 40 poems. Does your Foundation have any kind of fundraising activities that could help a mentally ill person with the cost of publishing a poetry book?

Even if your Foundation cannot help me in any way about the things I talked about in this letter, I still wanted to send you my poems so you could enjoy them, and I am curious to know more about you (Nathaniel.)

Even if your Foundation cannot help me in any way, please write back and tell me how you like my poems.

Nancy K.

*Nancy K. shared two beautiful poems with me entitled "Illumination" and "Madness." Maybe, one day, we will see her poetic works in print.

To NAAF,

Thank you so much for sending me your newsletter. Please continue to do so. Please do not be afraid to send anything else related to him, including requests for donations. I cannot forget the effect he had on my own life. Thirty years ago, I ran the halfway house (Hill House) that he was released into when he left Fairhill Psychiatric Hospital. He and I talked about classical music then, so I knew Nathaniel was different from any other client I would ever have. By the way, I also had Harry Barnoff as my own double bass teacher at the time, and Harry and I still talk frequently about those days. When I left Hill House, I was given two broken portions of the stairway banister as a going-away present by the residents (long story but it makes sense). I still have them. Should you find an interest in them, I would be happy to donate them to you.

Jon

Hi, my name is SV! I saw the movie *The Soloist*! My girlfriend is taking an English class and she is reading the book and I am helping her! I would love for her to meet him! Nathaniel! Do you think it could be possible! We live in Los Angeles, California! Thank you!!!

To Whom It May Concern:

Just finished watching the movie *The Soloist* and was very touched by Nathaniel's story. Is it possible to get an update on him? Is he still living in the apt? Does he get treatment for his mental issue? Any info will be much appreciated. God Bless.

Best Regards, Flavia

My husband is a psychiatry resident at the Center for Behavioral Medicine (CBM), Kansas City, MO. Few weeks ago, a 40-year-old homeless female patient was admitted to the CBM facility. She was diagnosed with schizophrenia several years ago. She almost had an undergraduate degree in music major, from Indiana University. She is a concert violinist. At present, we have given her our daughter's ¾ size violin. Twice a day she plays violin for about 30 minutes. I would like to find any help, information about how we continue her playing of violin with some assistance. I inquired for a violin cost which is truly for a beginner and its cost is $750.00. At the moment, it is very high for us. Do you suggest any place where we can find her inexpensive violin? Also, way to continue her music advancement or playing in a group? Playing violin is truly helping her calm down. Any help / suggestion will be truly appreciated.

Thank you, H & M S

    My name is Corbin. I am 12 years old. I am a huge fan of Nathaniel and I was wondering if he could send me an autograph. Thank you.

Dear Jennifer and Nathaniel,

    I am really sorry to worry you with any problem when I know you might be busy with work at the moment. My name is AJ, a Sierra Leone by nationality, based in the United Kingdom. I am a big fan of Nathaniel and appreciate the work your Foundation is doing keeping up public awareness about Mental health. Just wondering if there is any plan for your organization to expand to new regions. I would like to register your organization in Sierra Leone and work with the foundation. I hope we can all be part of creating a world in which every man and child has the opportunity to enjoy good health and live in peace. I hope to hear from you soon.

Sincerely, AJ

WOW! Nathaniel Ayers has become an inspiration to me! I read *The Soloist* and saw the movie and I got inspired by him! Mr. Steve Lopez could you write about how he is doing? I would like to know (I am a violinist too, but not as amazing as Mr. Ayers) One day I'd like to see him in person, you should bring him to the east coast and see Juilliard again! I am going to apply there from college and tell me how he's doing. I would like to know his string brand. I fell in love listening to his violin ...Best Regards!
P.S. Please could you make a sequel to *The Soloist*? And bring him over to the Kennedy Center any day.

Patrick L.

Hello,

My name is Andrej P., and I am writing to you on behalf of Speakers, s r o, a Slovakia-based speakers bureau

I'm aware this is an unusual request, but I would very much appreciate it if you could send me the email address of Ms. Ayers-Moore as our company would very much like to engage in cooperation with her as a speaker and could not get in touch with her through other means. Alternatively, I would be very indebted if you could notify her of our request. I think she might appreciate this chance as well. Many thanks for considering this odd request. Have a nice time.

Best regards,
Andrej P.

My reading club is discussing *The Soloist* on Wednesday. I would like to know how Nathaniel is doing now. Did he ever agree to medication? Is he still sleeping at LAMP? I loved reading about him and was inspired by his story. I was also happy to learn about your foundation. I will pass on information to my book discussion group.

LE, New Albany-Floyd County Public Library

Good Afternoon,

    I recently watched *The Soloist* and became aware of NAAF. I was moved by the story and was hoping I could offer some help. I have a flute that I used when I was a music student in high school some years ago. As I have not played in quite some time and was moved by the foundation's mission. I wondered if there was a way to donate used instruments for those who are assisted by NAAF services.
    If not, I understand, and will try to arrange a financial contribution instead, but wanted to know if this was an option first.

Many Thanks,
Mike L.

NATHANIEL

AYERS

Recessional

A Call to Action: This Is How You Can Help!

Our concept for the Nathaniel Anthony Ayers Foundation began in 2008 after the publication of Steve Lopez's book about Nathaniel called *The Soloist: A Lost Dream, an Unlikely Friendship, and the Redemptive Power of Music*. We were in talks about a movie when my husband, Jerry, said to me, "Do you see what's happening? Your mom's dream is coming true. Here is your catch while you have some attention." I knew it was difficult to get the public and people in positions of power to take an earnest look at the dire needs of the mental health community. After all, I had watched my mom devote her life to that exact purpose from the moment doctors had diagnosed her "Tony" with schizophrenia. She had dragged me along with her when I was a child, and although I saw her get frustrated, she never threw in the towel despite the lack of support and stonewalling she received.

Jerry, in his own way, inspired me to take advantage of the light finally shining on the issue which had driven my mother for so long; her dream was to provide the mental health community with tangible resources and information about how to find the help they needed whether it was food, shelter, clothing, toiletries, medical care, support, or love. She wanted fair treatment for the mentally ill, like everyone else, and better treatment for them than her son had received. Mom's passion had grown in me, creating a desire to develop an organization which would adhere to the basic tenets she had set up, incorporate what I had learned about therapy through the arts, and would affect a larger footprint than I could create out of my home.

I knew I needed help to build the vision consuming me, so my husband, Jerry, and I had recruited my brother-in-law, Tony, to help. The movie had fueled the fire in me to effect change for the mental health community, and I knew I had to begin going public for our cause, while I could. I had hoped to attract those in need in the mental health community who needed the kind of help I believed I could offer.

We had an opportunity to directly address a need and attract attention for our cause when we attended a screening of *The Soloist* at the Cedar Lee Theater in Cleveland, Ohio to a sold-out theater of 300 in 2009. The Magnolia Clubhouse hosted the screening and the proceeds from the event supported the Clubhouse's center for psychosocial rehabilitation. Cleveland appreciated the opportunity to see a Hollywood film about one of their own which was clear at the end of the movie when the crowd jumped to their feet and erupted with clapping and cheers. We conducted a question and answer session afterwards and the simplest question from the audience stumped us: "How can we help?" I could not answer. I had not yet thought past our own, small circle of involvement.

We were novices back then — especially me— and had not considered that the movie would light a fire motivating a vast amount of people other than ourselves to rally behind our cause which my Mom had birthed decades before. That simple question has stuck in my mind since that night, as you can imagine, pushing me to stay the course like my mom did. It is easy to answer now, but the answer is not easy to implement. The answer requires a world-wide mindset change and a willingness to affect change outside the security of our individual bubbles. That answer seems daunting and enormous when I consider the magnitude of it. But a wildfire can start with just a small spark, can it not?

I believe my mom understood this concept when she invited Ms. Powell to live in our home and said, "I am doing for Ms. Powell what I would like for someone to do for Tony." She was the spark that started a flame, and her dream was the catalyst creating a wildfire of positive change for a multitude of lives. She believed the seed of help she planted would one day pay it forward for her son. I also believe Steve Lopez's entry into my brother's life was the harvest which sprung up from the seed planted by my mom in Ms. Powell's life.

Mom's advocacy had begun by having me write letters to politicians in Cleveland hoping to gain allies for her mission. She soon realized that politics is a slow, sometimes selfish, game and she was getting nowhere quickly with them. I continued to write letters, but Mom decided she could take immediate, direct, tangible action and effect change right in her community by **doing** while she was waiting for politicians to catch up. I remember riding with her to collect information, pamphlets, and brochures from multiple centers whose purpose was to help people like my brother and families like ours. Additionally, she brought ladies home for lunch, gave them clothes, styled their hair, and chatted with them like the equals they were. My mom helped them feel respected and valued, despite their diagnosis. She had a special place in her heart to help others – a trait she passed on to me.

    I had always wanted to and continue to want to pursue Mom's dream of helping those suffering from a mental health condition and their families receive respectful and fair treatment and to receive the resources they deserve as a human right. The timing seemed right in the wake of the book and subsequent movie release, so *The Nathaniel Anthony Ayers Foundation (NAAF)* was born. It was a simple concept for me, at first. I wanted us to meet basic needs of the mentally ill, many of whom were homeless.

    I spent time and money, though not enough, to pack book bags to distribute which held items like socks, t-shirts, blankets, soap, toothpaste, toothbrushes, etcetera, and a bible. Most of us take those things for granted, it seemed like a trivial sentiment to some. I can promise you that, tangible sentiment, however, is the only thing that matters when you do not have it. It was a tough challenge to get people to agree with that concept. Those backpacks filled with love and basic items would allow many individuals to feel like someone cared about and accepted them, even if it were only for a moment. That seemingly simple act turned out to be a huge undertaking, especially once we decided to get serious about structuring the Foundation and focusing more on healing through group Music and Art Therapy. That dream got pushed back because we could not keep up with it.

    We recruited many individuals to help us, along the way, but realized everyone had their own ideas on how NAAF should have functioned. We ended up deciding on a mission statement as we fumbled around getting our bearings on how to best help the demographic we wanted to serve. Our mission became, "to support art programs at mental health and arts organizations that serve the mentally ill. We place a special emphasis on programs that serve the artistically gifted." We passionately believed and still believe that artistic expression increases health and wellness within the mentally ill. We also quickly learned it takes a tremendous amount of time and money to set up an organization like NAAF.

    We had asked for financial backing and found a huge supporter in the California Endowment. We also received support from other organizations and individuals, mostly on the west coast, who wanted to help because they loved Nathaniel and could identify with his story. It seemed that the money we received was never enough though and everything had a cost. One such cost that had an excellent return on investment was my opportunity to travel and deliver speeches which raised awareness and supplied verbal resources and support for the mental health community.

I always enjoyed arriving the day before a speech and sitting with the organization that had brought me, so I could learn about them, their needs, and what was working for them. The mutual sharing of stories, building relationships, and learning how to work together to further the mission for the mental health community blessed me. Many people asked about Nathaniel which gave me the chance to share what had and had not worked for us. It always seemed to come back to Music and Art Therapy, though. I knew, firsthand, how much it helped, I advocated for it, and the places I visited that had therapy through the arts seemed to be the most successful. The cost I could have never accounted for when founding NAAF, though, was the disingenuousness of some in my inner circle.

Many of the people who had joined our organization had great ideas about trying to capitalize on the popularity of the book and movie. Of course, that publicity helped, but the big vision for the Foundation began to steer the organization away from the most basic principles of my original vision. I began to realize the glamour and sensationalism of the movie had attracted many people to NAAF, which was incredible, but not all of them were the right people for the job. NAAF was becoming a bureaucratic bog, and I felt like it had become more talk than action. Eventually, interest in the book and movie began to fade away and interest in the Nathaniel Anthony Ayers Foundation followed. Those who had joined our mission with a flurry of excitement started leaving when the dust settled, until I found myself nearly alone in my endeavor.

  My brother-in-law, Tony, having moved to a new city, continued to help the best he could from a distance. I remain full of gratitude with his loyalty and dedication. Then Jerry died in 2011. By the time these events took place, I was wearing two hats as the Founder and Executive Director. I kept the Foundation and mission rolling for as long as I could, but I felt incomplete and like something was missing. The exodus of employees and volunteers had begun to crumble the foundation of NAAF in the long shadows of the movie.

  I was struggling to keep the Foundation above water, practically on my own. I could not supply a steady paycheck for any of the people who wandered in and out of the Foundation. I knew I needed to seriously restructure the Nathaniel Anthony Ayers Foundation if it was to survive and continue to help people and make a real difference. Lacking help and resources I needed to keep pressing forward, the Nathaniel Anthony Ayers Foundation ceased to exist as it had in the early days.

In hindsight, I realize I made plenty of mistakes in the early days of building the Foundation, and one of the biggest was not sticking to Mom's dream or mine. "Bigger is always better" is a philosophy I had never believed in, and our journey through the school of hard knocks with the Foundation confirmed my feelings on that philosophy. Even though our large Foundation set up a few plans I felt were beneficial to the mental health community, I learned the K.I.S.S. way is usually the best way to effect lasting change. "Keep it simple, Stupid" may seem like a childish or harsh philosophy, but it reminds me to stick with the basics, first. I never want to forget the enormous meaning and value in a small backpack filled with toiletries and love for a few, consistently, over an enormous organization trudging along at a snail's pace barely ever effecting loveless, slight change in the lives of many.

I think about Mom's efforts often, to this day, and my desire to get back on track with Mom's mission and the Nathaniel Anthony Ayers Foundation still drives me. I eat, sleep, think, dream, and work toward this every day of my life. I will always hold a special place in my heart to help people with mental health conditions and their families, just like Mom did. Though the Foundation did help some, it did not help the way I had originally wanted it to.

My experiences with the Foundation in the early years helped me realize that there were reasons for the ideas God had planted about the Foundation in my mind and heart. His ways and thoughts have always been and will always be higher than my ways or thoughts. I want to complete the restructuring I had envisioned for NAAF by taking it back to the basics where it should have been the entire time starting with its new name – Friends of Ayers Foundation (FOA). My mistakes and experiential wisdom have given me confidence to know what I need to do better with the Foundation this time, so it will make a lasting impact on the mental health community.

Firstly, I want to see the Foundation return to doing hands-on, tangible things like stuffing and distributing backpacks or even passing out water or cups of coffee. Small gestures like these easily open the door for conversations with people suffering from a mental health condition, the homeless, and their families. Open dialogue helps uncover real needs and paves the way for us to supply pertinent information to meet those needs.

Secondly, I want to create an avenue and safe space for people to share their stories. My travels with NAAF in the early days helped me understand the power our stories hold which is why I decided to write this book. The downside is that I am only one person and it has taken a long time for me to write down my story. Vulnerability like this is extremely difficult, but I did it and so can others. The upside is for my story to spark a raging fire of storytelling within the mental health community, helping all of us in this fight to understand we are not alone.

Thirdly, I hope to attract volunteers and then, hopefully, paid employees, so that the Friends of Ayers

Foundation can reach its full potential. I pray these people have a genuine concern for the mentally ill and their families. I need for these volunteers and employees to grasp the basic vision of the Friends of Ayers Foundation and be committed to staying the course of our basic mission. I want these people to be trailblazers in and out of the mental health community, like me, who fight to make people listen to the needs of the mentally ill and their families, and offer information about valuable resources to make this life more manageable for them. I also hope they are eager to write letters, roll up their sleeves to stuff backpacks, organize fundraisers, and petition for funds and help from private businesses, and cities, counties, and states, at all levels of government.

  Fourthly, I hope and pray that Friends of Ayers can get the funding it needs to help provide information on how to start and grow and Music and Art Therapy groups in mental health facilities everywhere. And if possible, eventually FOA can create a Music and Arts Therapy endowment fund whose purpose is to give financial aid to programs trying to get off the ground so they can buy music, instruments, hire teachers and fund concerts, art walks, and live theatre productions. I imagine funding for this aspect of the Foundation's mission will come from various fundraising efforts like an Annual FOA Golf Tournament down to something as simple as grassroots fundraisers like bake sales.

I have been talking about this book and my vision to restructure NAAF to FOA for quite a while. I feel blessed it is finally coming to fruition for two reasons. One, people can see my genuine heart, my honesty and realness. Two, I believe people are going to step forward who have a desire to work with me to build strong, safe bridges between the mental health community and the rest of the world, closing the disparity gap, and helping the mentally ill to become the widely respected citizens they deserve to be. I envision FOA spanning the breadth of the United States as a bright beacon of hope, strength, courage, and love.

Here is how you can help Nathaniel, me, and thousands of others like us:

1. Learn to "Hear the Music." Change your mindset toward the mentally ill, homeless, their friends, and their loved ones. The stigma will only stop if everyone owns their thinking and actions. You can get help to learn how to change your mindset and become #StigmaFree at www.CureStigma.org. You can also learn to #StopStigma by visiting my blog at www.HeartheMusicWeb.blog or www.FriendsofAyers.org. I know from experience, changing your mindset is not a feeling — it is a choice.

*Decide to "Hear the Music" of others.
Then teach others around you to "Hear the
Music" too.*

2. Donate items like hygiene products, clothes, instruments, art supplies, etcetera to homeless shelters and mental health centers.

   *What daily thing can you not live without?
   Donate that.*

3. Volunteer your time or services at homeless shelters and mental health centers. Some residents at those facilities are grateful for conversation with humans who treat them as equals and others receive help from art or music lessons, board game or basketball partners, haircuts, manicures, or outings.

   *What activity or amenity brings you joy?
   Donate that.*

4. Give financial support to organizations like the Friends of Ayers Foundation, the National Alliance on Mental Illness, the American Music Therapy Association, The National Coalition for the Homeless, and La Casa Mental Health Service in Long Beach, CA. The average cost of one meal for homeless in a shelter is $3.

How much do you spend a day to get your coffee/tea/sports drink fix?
Donate that.

5. Hire a speaker/expert to come talk with your clubs and organizations to raise awareness about mental health and homelessness which could empower all around you to change their mindsets to be able to "Hear the Music" of others or get help if they struggle with mental health issues, personally. I want to continue traveling and speaking and am eager to help more people to learn to "Hear the Music." *You may contact me for speaking engagements through The American Program Bureau, Inc.* (www.apbspeakers.com) *and by registering with my blog* (www.HeartheMusicWeb.blog) *or the Foundation website* (www.FriendsOfAyers.org). Please be on the lookout for FOA's website facelift happening during this book's publishing!

6. Share your POSITIVE story to help #StopStigma associated with mental illness by emailing me at FriendsofAyers@gmail.com. Your submission should be 500 words or less[2]*. I will include it in the *free* "Hear the Music" publication. I am seeking two kinds of stories:

---

[2] *Stories may be edited for length to ensure they meet publication requirements.*

a. I would love to hear your "Nathaniel Story," if you have known or met Nathaniel at any time in your life. Please submit the POSITIVE story about you and Nathaniel by typing "MY NATHANIEL STORY" in the subject line of your email.

b. I also want to hear the POSITIVE stories of how you can "HEAR the MUSIC" of a loved one diagnosed with a mental illness. Please submit the POSITIVE story about you and your loved one by typing "THE MUSIC OF MY LOVED ONE" in the subject line of your email.

My brother, Nathaniel, and I need people like you to stand strong with us and with people like us, if we ever hope to create lasting, POSITIVE change for the, often overlapping, mentally ill and homeless communities. Please join our advocacy by putting into *action* the steps I shared and encourage others to do the same. It is time for all of us to learn to "HEAR the MUSIC!"

Jennifer

Appendix A: Blended Chaos

These memories are meant to give insight into the turmoil we faced as we were learning to function as one, blended, Mangrum family instead of two, distinct families.

My elementary and my siblings' junior high schools were on the same street after we moved to Churchill Avenue, so we walked to school. Everyone went their own way when we moved to Churchill; or maybe it was the step sibling strife which made us try to keep our distance as much as possible.

June was the oldest and nicest of the four Mangrum children. She was soft spoken, and I never saw her do anything to hurt anyone, unlike her siblings. It was not long after we moved in before she moved out, got married, and had her first child. She would come back to visit, but dreadful things were happening in the house, by then, she was not aware of. For example, my stepbrothers, Bubba and Michael, were in one of the bedrooms one day talking and laughing about something with me and my stepsister, Barbara. Suddenly, Michael jabbed me in the buttocks with a long hat pin and it stuck. It caught me off guard and hurt physically and emotionally. The three of them stood there looking at me as I pulled it out. By the smirk on Bubba's face, I believe he had coerced Michael to stick me.

Michael was nice to me after that, but he never apologized. He won a contest for delivering the most newspapers on his route and shared with me his winnings, a brand-new bike with the latest style banana seat, possibly as penance for hurting me. I appreciated the gift, but I never got over the feeling of betrayal nor did I turn my back on either of them again.

Not long after that, I was standing in Mom's doorway talking to her when something pricked her hand as she fluffed her pillow getting ready for bed. She recoiled in surprise, carefully patted the pillow, and was stuck by something again. She removed the pillowcase to discover several hatpins lodged in it. I was shocked, and at once knew who had put those pins in her pillow. Mom knew too, but we did not discuss it with each other. I did not hear about further threats of harm to her after that. She was a smart and savvy lady, so I have no doubt she took care of it even though she did not tell me how. It was just a few years ago I shared "the story of the hatpins" with June and she told me, "Bubba did that to me too."

Barbara and Del dealt with their share of friction too. Barbara would come home from work, and on many occasions, she would go into Mom's room to talk for a while. I was in Mom's room one night when Del worked up the nerve to walk in and demand the truth on why Barbara could come in and chat with Mom, but she could not. Mom said, "You can come in." Del replied, "Barbara said I wasn't allowed." Mom looked so disappointed.

After that, Mom demanded privacy whenever Del came to her room to chat. I could overhear them talking and laughing which made me happy for Del. She had been hurting thinking her own mother did not want to talk to her based on what Barbara had told her. Barbara knocked on the door one night and Mom said, "We will be out in a minute." I could see that made Del feel better, but it bothered me it had to happen that way, only to prove a point to Barbara. I also remember another incident between Del and Barbara, vividly.

Barbara, some of her friends, and I were all standing in front of our house when Nathaniel and Del came out. Barbara decided to introduce everyone, but she overlooked Del. The expression of hurt on Del's face made me hurt too. Then Del leaned against the car and Barbara "accidentally" slammed the door on Del's hand. Del's hand could only be set free by opening the door. She was in pain but did not cry in front of the others. She shook her hand and went into the house. Del had cheerleading captain tryouts the next day and pushed through, despite the pain.

I never fully understood Del and Barbara's friction when I was a kid and chalked it up to "normal" family stuff.

Favoritism was also something "normal" in our blended family. I remember starting to leave our house once when I heard my stepfather call Michael downstairs. "Come here. Hurry up," he said as I reached the bottom of the stairs. I got down in time to see him handing Michael spending money. They stopped and stared at me, but I never said a word. My stepfather did not offer the same to me, and I left the house feeling disappointed. Betrayal, disappointment, and even fear were feelings my siblings and I felt for a while in the Mangrum house.

Once, I heard Michael and Del arguing in the basement. Their voices were elevating, so I ran down the steps to see what was happening. Just as I made it to the last step, I heard a thump and saw a meat cleaver stuck in the wall. Del stood there, first frozen in disbelief, then she started crying. She became enraged, and I had to stop her from going after Michael. I thought, "What else is he capable of if he can throw a meat cleaver that close to Del's head?" Michael bolted up the steps, partially in fear of Del and partially because of what he had done. Del started screaming, "Did you see that? Did you see that?" I could only eek out, "Yes, I did."

I was shocked and frightened. I remember Mom, our stepfather (whom we called Dad or Daddy), Del, and Michael later met in the kitchen to discuss the meat cleaver incident. I stood at the top of the steps and listened to the whole conversation. It was an intense conversation, though no one seemed upset. I remember feeling dizzy thinking about Michael running to pull the meat cleaver out of the wall. I was physically sick knowing he could do such a thing and even sicker seeing how close it had come to hitting Del in the head. They made Michael apologize then everything went blurry for me after that. Similar incidents happened periodically without the meat cleavers.

One day before Nathaniel's diagnosis, our neighbor came by our house asking for empty pop bottles to turn in for money. We always had plenty sitting on our back porch. I was saying "sure" as I saw Nathaniel walking up the driveway turning red with anger. I did not know what had happened, but saw he was coming for Russell. I remember Nathaniel wore a green zip up sweater with beige stripes, perfectly matched green slacks, and green suede shoes with no socks. His clothing still sticks out to me, because I thought he would never fight in those clothes. I was wrong; he was ready to fight.

Russell started saying, "I'm sorry, Nate. Man, I'm sorry!" My brother said, "Call me a name now!" Russell cried out, "No, I'm not ever going to call you a name again." The next thing I know I saw blood gushing from Russell's head as he tried, desperately, to get away. Nathaniel was so angry; he meant to prove a point and I could not get him to stop. Russell finally got away and ran home. Unfortunately for Nathaniel, Russell's brothers did not take too well to that beating and were spoiling for retaliation. Nathaniel probably knew what was coming next, so he did not stick around to find out.

I ran over to Russell's house as soon as Nathaniel left, since I was friends with his sister, and told her the true account of what had happened. Russell had told his brothers a bloody tale about Nathaniel jumping him for no reason. I heard Russell's big brother say, "That don't sound like Nate." Everyone knew fighting was out of character for Nathaniel, but it still looked like he was on the verge of hunting Nathaniel down. My friend and I pleaded with Russell's older brother. She said, "Russell was calling Nate names." Her big brother turned and said, "you didn't tell me that, Russell!" Russell finally confessed that some other boys were teasing Nate and he joined in. The big brother told Russell he was "dead wrong." He was still upset about his little brother's battered face, so they went looking for Nathaniel anyway. My friend and I cried and begged them to not hurt Nathaniel. There was nothing else I could do, so I went home.

Mom was home when I got there. She had already heard about what went down, so we hopped in the car to look for Nathaniel. Our car met Russell's mom's car on the corner at the end of our street. Mom said, "I am so sorry. I heard about what happened. Have you seen Nathaniel?" Mom did not realize Russell's family was looking for Nathaniel to beat the pulp out of him. Russell's mom screamed, "No. I haven't seen him, and you better hope I don't!" My friend was trying to disappear in the backseat as her mother showed a knife to my mom. Mom warned, "You better not touch my son!"

Everything happened so quickly and both cars sped away in opposite directions. We could not find Nathaniel after searching until late, so we went home. Nathaniel was already home, and our stepbrother, Bubba, had just walked in too. Bubba was on leave from the Army which worked out perfectly for Nathaniel. Bubba worked out all the time and had a strong physique, so he intimidated the neighborhood boys. Bubba went over to Russell's house and smoothed things out, somehow. Russell did not tease nor call Nathaniel names again. I believe they often teased Nathaniel which partially explained why he got heavily into music at that time.

I remember one Saturday morning just like it was yesterday. I was on our back porch turned bedroom. There were some neighborhood boys out back laughing loudly and talking with Bubba and Nathaniel. They were having a pushup battle which, of course, was Bubba's thing. He had the advantage since he could easily do several hundred pushups. One of the boys named Gary had just finished doing pushups and the other boys congratulated him on a job well done. Another boy tried, but no one could beat Bubba's record. Then they challenged Nathaniel. I prayed for him to "do a lot of pushups." He pressed out about 30, jumped up and started crying. He looked so distraught it broke my heart. All the boys laughed at him, so he ran off. I knew it had little to do with the push-ups because he could have done more, physically. Something prohibited him from keeping it together, though.

I was so angry with those boys I ran downstairs to defend Nathaniel's honor by pushing one of them. Bubba protected me from the neighborhood boys while I gave them a piece of my mind, which they thought was funny. I felt so badly for Nathaniel and waited a long time for him to come in the house. He was distant when he finally came in. That whole scenario pierced my soul and I hurt, deeply, with Nathaniel. I was so young, at the time. I could not understand his discombobulation with that situation. Years of personal and professional experience eventually helped me process and understand how mental illness greatly affects one's ability to respond to stressful situations like the pushup contest, Although Nathaniel had not been diagnosed yet, I have wondered how deeply his mental health was affecting him, at this point. This situation seemed to plunge Nathaniel even deeper into the music he was growing to love.

I had a recurring dream when I was a pre-teen where I was walking then would start running, suddenly. When I looked back, I would fly into the air, still running as quickly as I could. Sometimes, my brother and sister would be standing there watching me fly higher and higher. I had that dream for over a year or longer. It seemed like it went on forever. The next day I would be tired, dragging, and get in trouble for moving too slowly as I got ready for school. I shared my dream with Mom, frustrated by what it might mean. I remember how she turned around, looked me right in the eyes when I explained the dream, and said, "they will catch up." I was not sure what she meant, but it felt like a ton of bricks fell from my shoulders.

One night, after telling Mom about that dream, I had a different dream. I dreamed my brother and I were running on the ground, and he was ahead of me. I tried running more quickly to catch him when I elevated into the air. He never looked back or up at me, and I could not catch him in my dream that night.

I had another dream in which I was attending a church service in an old, shack-like building. Nathaniel, Del, and my stepbrother, Michael, were there too, though we were not sitting together. Everyone was quiet and people were fanning themselves because of the heat. Nathaniel closed his eyes. (There is a scene in *The Soloist* movie where Nathaniel closes his eyes, and you begin to see the flashing of colors. That scene reminded me of this dream!) I remember waking and thinking, "Okay. I did not have a dream about running, but what was that about?" I only had that dream one time and did not share it with Mom. She later asked me if I still had the "running dream." I told her no, and she replied, "Sharing freed you. You can share your dreams with me."

I cannot know with certainty what the dreams meant if anything at all. I believed her, though, when Mom said, "They will catch up," since my brother was running ahead of me in my last dream. I felt comforted having my shared dreams in common with Mom.

Appendix B: The Girls

Nathaniel was a very handsome boy who grew to be a handsome man. There were many reasons why the girls found Nathaniel infatuating which is probably why so many in our community chased after him. He was a dapper dresser for his age, made the honor roll, played football, sang, played in the school orchestra and was in the drama club. He would sometimes join the older kids at house parties.

Del and our step siblings threw a house party one night, and I decided to "sneak" in with our Super 8mm motion picture camera to make a movie of the party. I use the word "sneak" loosely, since this film munching camera was massive. Unfortunately for me, in my quest to make movie magic, I stumbled upon Nathaniel kissing a girl. I decided I had had enough partying after that discovery and told Del what I saw on my way back upstairs. Del broke up their little kissing session, and I am sure Nathaniel never knew I had seen him. Despite all the attention he received, I never saw Nathaniel show too much interest in any one girl until Darla came along.

Darla was a smart girl with long black hair, a slender build, light complexion, and a sweet personality. It was easy to see why Nathaniel loved her. No one else seemed to matter when he was with Darla. Mom liked Darla too. Our mother had a brand-new, white, late 1960s Oldsmobile she would let Nathaniel use to take Darla out on dates.

Nathaniel and Darla ended up in a McDonald's parking lot in east Cleveland during one of their dates where a group of white men approached them mistaking Darla as white. The thought of a white girl being in the car with my brother enraged that group, so the boy closest to Nathaniel's window threatened him with a gun while another began beating the car with an axe. They were able to get away, but the incident shook Nathaniel, and Mom was extremely upset by what had happened. I vividly remember seeing the eerie axe marks on the hood and side of Mom's car.

Somehow, Mom got the names of the guys who did the damage, sued them, and the court made them repair the damage to her car. Darla ended up breaking it off with Nathaniel not long after that which broke his heart. I am not sure what caused the breakup, but I know she married young and quickly had a child. I hope Darla had a wonderful, full life, and I wish Nathaniel could have seen her again. I wonder how Nathaniel's life might be different if he and Darla had gotten married and had kids.

During one of his stays at home, on Churchill, Nathaniel set up shop in the attic so he could play bass for hours on end. A pleasant girl stopped by to see him one day, so we told her she could go ahead upstairs to see Nathaniel. She left less than 30 minutes later looking like she had seen a ghost but did not tell us what happened. I went up to the attic to check on him, because I could still hear him playing. I entered the attic and saw what most likely sent his friend running. Nathaniel stopped playing and gave me a look that sent shivers down my spine. He was likely in the beginning stages of his diagnosis then, but we did not know. We only knew he was acting differently. I am not sure why we did not warn her of his turbulent moods before we sent her up. We were in denial at that time, I guess.

I drove Nathaniel to see a girl once who lived in a very affluent neighborhood with her family. I waited in the car during Nathaniel's short visit with her because her family would not even speak to me. I remember the girl having long hair, a full figure and slurred speech because of a medication she was taking. The girl's parents asked us not to return and the girl cried as we drove away. It was a strange trip and a long ride back home. Nathaniel was so excited and upbeat on the way to her house, so sullen on our way home. I am almost positive he was compliant with his medication during this time.

I was a student at Kent State University when Nathaniel managed to make his way to campus to visit me. He had been interested in becoming an orchestra student and fared well during his visit. He ended up not becoming a student at Kent State, nor did he talk much about it after the visit, but he did continue to visit me. My friend, Carol, saw Nathaniel during one of his visits, and thought he was handsome. I gave Carol a ride home to Cleveland during one of our school breaks, and she told me during that ride she wanted to meet Nathaniel. I had no idea how to explain his health to her, so I set up a meeting between the two of them for that night.

Nathaniel and I started down the road to Carol's when he asked if he could drive. I thought it would be ok since he seemed to be doing well, so we switched seats and he drove. He pulled out slowly then I suddenly slammed back into the seat as he stomped his foot on the gas. I thanked God for miraculously clearing the way for us as we sped down the street. We were going so fast I thought we were going to die. I screamed, "Anthony, stop! Slow down! You are going to kill us!" After a minute, whatever had overtaken him was gone as quickly as it had come, and he carefully drove the rest of the way to Carol's apartment. She did not notice his behavior, but she saw I was a nervous wreck and asked if I was okay.

    Carol and Nathaniel tried to hold a conversation, but she thought Nathaniel was only trying to be funny when he said things that did not make sense. Carol did not have a clue what was going on with Nathaniel which troubled me. I am sure Nathaniel's mental health caused a disconnect that day which is why he did not feel attracted to her, even though she was a kind, sweet person. We did not stay long, and on the way to our car Nathaniel said, "I'll drive." Then he laughed when I angrily replied, "No you won't! I will drive!"

    Our short ride home seemed terribly long as Nathaniel stared out the front window, deep in thought, and I was quietly hurting on the inside. Somehow, I downplayed my brother's illness in my mind and thought Carol might be able to help him. I wished for Nathaniel and Carol to be happy together, but I knew deep down that was not going to happen. Any relationship they would have developed would have been short lived and a disaster, most likely.

I spent time in denial and refused to hold on to moments like that day where a discombobulated moment of psychosis forced him to drive out of control threatening our safety. I could see how subdued Nathaniel was on the ride home and I desperately wanted him to be okay. I suggested we stop by Aunt Willa and Uncle Howard's since spending time with them usually helped him to feel better. He curtly replied, "No," then fell asleep. I longed to rescue him from the road he was traveling.

After he became ill, Nathaniel seemed to be attracted exclusively to white women with some sort of mental illness. Nine times out of ten, he met them at a mental health facility. He often had his lady friends call me while he was with them. They would tell me, "I've heard so much about you." Nathaniel had more ladies who wanted to be his friend after the release of the movie, *The Soloist*.

One lady had some good qualities but was amid her own gigantic battle. She helped him with the huge task of cleaning his apartment. I saw them interact once and realized how toxic and dangerous their relationship was. She did manage to get him to the hospital one Christmas day when he was sick. He had to stay overnight, and Steve Lopez left his own family dinner to be with Nathaniel in the hospital. It was a miracle how things worked out that day to help my brother, and I will be forever grateful to thanked God for miraculously clearing the way for us as we sped down the street. We were going so fast I thought we were going to die. I screamed, "Anthony, stop! Slow down! You are going to kill us!" After a minute, whatever had overtaken him was gone as quickly as it had come, and he carefully drove the rest of the way to Carol's apartment. She did not notice his behavior, but she saw I was a nervous wreck and asked if I was okay.

    Carol and Nathaniel tried to hold a conversation, but she thought Nathaniel was only trying to be funny when he said things that did not make sense. Carol did not have a clue what was going on with Nathaniel which troubled me. I am sure Nathaniel's mental health caused a disconnect that day which is why he did not feel attracted to her, even though she was a kind, sweet person. We did not stay long, and on the way to our car Nathaniel said, "I'll drive." Then he laughed when I angrily replied, "No you won't! I will drive!"

    Our short ride home seemed terribly long as Nathaniel stared out the front window, deep in thought, and I was quietly hurting on the inside. Somehow, I downplayed my brother's illness in my mind and thought Carol might be able to help him. I wished for Nathaniel and Carol to be happy together, but I knew deep down that was not going to happen. Any relationship they would have developed would have been short lived and a disaster, most likely.

I spent time in denial and refused to hold on to moments like that day where a discombobulated moment of psychosis forced him to drive out of control threatening our safety. I could see how subdued Nathaniel was on the ride home and I desperately wanted him to be okay. I suggested we stop by Aunt Willa and Uncle Howard's since spending time with them usually helped him to feel better. He curtly replied, "No," then fell asleep. I longed to rescue him from the road he was traveling.

After he became ill, Nathaniel seemed to be attracted exclusively to white women with some sort of mental illness. Nine times out of ten, he met them at a mental health facility. He often had his lady friends call me while he was with them. They would tell me, "I've heard so much about you." Nathaniel had more ladies who wanted to be his friend after the release of the movie, *The Soloist*.

One lady had some good qualities but was amid her own gigantic battle. She helped him with the huge task of cleaning his apartment. I saw them interact once and realized how toxic and dangerous their relationship was. She did manage to get him to the hospital one Christmas day when he was sick. He had to stay overnight, and Steve Lopez left his own family dinner to be with Nathaniel in the hospital. It was a miracle how things worked out that day to help my brother, and I will be forever grateful to that woman and Steve for the way they cared for my brother.

A documentarian doing a piece on mental health/illness had spent a lot of time with my brother at one point. He called me often and it seemed she was with him quite a bit. I finally met her in the LAMP courtyard in LA and was surprised by how attractive she was. She was painfully overbearing though and wanted us to come to her home that evening. The negative vibe radiating from her bothered me, and Nathaniel seemed annoyed whenever she was around. In fact, no one felt comfortable going to her home, so we did not go. We told her we were overbooked – a legitimate excuse.

The woman called me the next day and said she "wanted us to come over to meet her aunt Nancy Wilson, a famous jazz singer." I am a Nancy Wilson fan, and I am sure Nathaniel is too, but we could not fit another visit in our schedule. I told her, "Oh, well. I am so sorry. Maybe we will get to meet her some other time." I did not tell Nathaniel who her relative was nor do I believe she mentioned it to him. He did not say much about her after that which is just as well, even though I did appreciate the time she had spent with him.

Some of the postings on his old apartment door clearly proved women were certainly on his mind, even though Nathaniel has not said much about his relationships, dating, or courtships, lately. I was visiting Nathaniel in L.A. once when he wistfully asked, "Why couldn't I have gotten married and had a family?" It was heart-wrenching to hear him say that and even harder for him to admit, I imagine. I never knew he felt that way until that moment, but he had such a big heart and always wanted the most from life. I did not know how to respond, but said, "I'm sorry. Maybe you will find someone." Then in a humorous way he said, "Maybe I'll have me a kid." I did not respond to that.

I used to wonder what Nathaniel's life would have been like had he been able to get married and have children. Would his children have been as beautiful, smart, and talented as he is? Would a family have made a difference in his recovery? Would they have joined me in my effort to help everyone "Hear the Music?" I cannot help wondering "what if," nor can I apologize. I hope my brother finds a lady friend he can confide in, care about and will care for him. I believe it is not too late.

Works Cited

Lopez, Steve. *The Soloist: A Lost Dream, an Unlikely Friendship, and the Redemptive Power of Music.* Penguin Publishing Group, 2010

Wright, J. (2009). *The Soloist.* Paramount Pictures

*"Decide to Hear the Music of others.
Then teach others to Hear the Music, too."*

Acknowledgements

There are so many people I want to thank for the love and support of my dear sweet brother, Nathaniel. I will start by thanking God for keeping Nathaniel safe and for His love and mercy in keeping Nathaniel alive during the many years he walked the streets.

Thank you, Nathaniel, for putting up with my ignorance, for making me a better person, and for teaching me there is more to life than what meets the eye. You taught me how wrong it is to be judgmental. What a valuable lesson to learn. I love you.

Next, I am thankful for my dear, wonderful mother, Floria Boone, who ALWAYS showed the strength, courage, and determination it took to be there for her son whom she absolutely loved, unconditionally. She was a fighter who stood her ground. I saw her frustration, but it invigorated her to stay on track and work even harder. She was ahead of her time and believed her generosity to others in the mental illness community would "Pay it Forward" for Nathaniel, and it did. Thank you to Momma and Stepdad, Donald Boone. RIP to both of you.

Thank you, Steve Lopez, for stepping up and taking a chance on Nathaniel. I appreciate how you always make people aware of the fact that not only did you help Nathaniel, but he helped you, too. It blesses me to hear him call you his "best friend." That, alone, is a huge breakthrough. Thank you for still trying to make a difference. It all helps.

I am grateful for all the people I have met who allowed Nathaniel to express himself.

Thank you to my sisters, Del in Cleveland, OH; Landi, in Georgia; and my half-sisters in Los Angeles, Lydia and Sarah.

To Jerry, my late husband (RIP) – I appreciate how you always encouraged me, and I am grateful to you for sharing your family. You never questioned my dreams; you only ever tried to make them come true.

To the Moore family – A special thank you for taking me and Nathaniel in, as blood family. Your love, support, acceptance, and encouragement has created a beautiful, lasting imprint on my soul.

My cousin, Greg, allowed me to vent and share my dreams with him about my many creative endeavors. He was always supportive and believed in me. No matter what I needed to make my dreams happen, he was always there, even when I did not expect it. Thank you, Greg, for never letting me down.

My brother-in-law, Tony, was one of the first people I contacted about building an organization to offer support to those who serve, in some capacity, the mentally ill community. He pushed to make that organization happen and diligently researches questions I need answered whenever I need help. Even though things are not as they should be, he has never given up on me. Thank you for staying in my corner.

Thank you to my close group of friends from John Hay High School who never questioned my brother's health. You probably do not even realize how much I appreciated our friendships and our mutual respect.

Thank you to my cousin Darryl for all your support and for listening to my long stories. I appreciate your efforts to help me with this book venture.

Stephanie and Cathy – I love you both and am thankful to you both for being there for us. Thank you for caring about Nathaniel and for your support.

Thank you, Dr. Barbara Lattimore, for all your support and for sharing your family.

Thank you to The Kelley family in Los Angeles for always giving me the opportunity to stay in your home and for reaching out to Nathaniel.

Bobby and Katrina Witbeck – you are family, and we love you for all you have done and continue to do. Nothing is too big! You are the best long-distance neighbors, ever.

Thank you to my cousin, Dr. Shondrika Moss-Bouldin, for helping me get out of the gate with my book and to lock down my title. Also, thanks to your dad, James Moss, the cop in Columbus!

Alysa Solomon (RIP) – you are gone too soon. You kept saying, "Get this book out there!" I am sorry I did not write it soon enough for you to finish reading it.

Thank you, Joann Pierce Martin and your wonderful husband, Gavin, for the sacrifices you have made to help Nathaniel, including coming to his party on YOUR birthday! It was a blessing to have you play with him on 60 Minutes.

You are so special, Dr. Elyn Saks, and I appreciate your support. Thank you for believing in me and reminding me I have an important story that needs sharing. I will be forever grateful for how you shared your life to encourage others, me included.

Thank you, Rebecca and Claire Phillips - the mother and daughter duo, I am happy to have you as friends.

To the National Alliance on Mental Illness – There are too many to list, but THANK YOU to all the NAMI offices in the U.S. I have met some amazing people and have learned so much from you! I can say we have remarkably similar goals. I pray that your message will continue, for as long as it is needed.

Thank you, Helen Dolas of Able ARTS Work (formerly Arts & Services for Disabled), for being another support system for Nathaniel, and thank you for being a friend to me.

Thank you, Ron Borczon of California State University, Northridge, for a great music therapy program and for reaching out to Nathaniel.

Many thanks to The Los Angeles Philharmonic Symphony Orchestra, past and present, including Joanne Pierce Martin, Robert Gupta, Benn Hung, and Lisa White.

Thank you, Adam Crane, for opening the door to Disney Concert Hall for Nathaniel. Now you are where he started. How about that?

Thank you, Professor Janise White, for allowing Nathaniel to play in the African American Chamber Orchestra in L.A.

Thank you, Joseph Russo, for playing with Nathaniel at the White House and for visiting him while you are in L.A. And a special thanks for being his friend while at Juilliard, and now.

Thank you to President Obama for inviting Nathaniel to play for the 20th American with Disability Act celebration at the White House.

Thank you to the MANY organizations that have invited me to share my story. I would love to come back to see how your programs are working out. I can honestly say that all whom I have had the privilege of visiting are doing SPLENDID work!

Ms. Julie, Charlotte, and Lorenzo – Thank you.

Ms. Priscilla - thanks for all your prayers!

Thank you to the entire Barnoff family, and especially to Mr. Harry Barnoff for believing in Nathaniel and making yourself available to speak with him on the phone!

Thank you, Cass Brewer, for all your kindness, ideas, and support. We will always be grateful.

Thank you, New City Church, for your love and prayers.

Thank you, Joyce, Renee, Jeannie, Tan, Betty, and Cynthia.

Thank you, Cassandra P., for the hard work you put in that will never be forgotten. Do not give up.

Thank you to Carol and Stephanie of TH Design for never giving up on me, even when the glass was empty.

Thank you to Ted for trying to build on the dream that was already in place. We appreciate your efforts and support.

Thank you, Gary F., and Russ K., for believing in the story enough to produce a film. I am sure you now see; it is more than a story. We appreciate you.

Thank you, to all those who cared enough to contribute in some way to help me on this journey. I say often, "It ain't over!"

I knew this was going to be hard once I started trying to say, "THANK YOU!" There have been so many people in my life who have helped me in more ways than I could ever count or list. Please know my gratitude is still the same, even if I forgot to mention you by name.

Thank you, Joshua, for being a respectful nephew to Nathaniel.

Last but not or ever least, thank you, Tracy Stokes and Stacie Sudkamp. You know my heart. You believed in me and believed that I should tell my story. As jumbled up as it was, you got it right, and I love you for "Hearing the Music."

About the Author

Jennifer Ayers-Moore is a mental health advocate, speaker, and author driven by her love for her brother, Nathaniel Ayers (a.k.a. *The Soloist*), a Juilliard scholarship recipient and classically trained, double bassist. Nathaniel was diagnosed with schizophrenia and, ultimately, became homeless. He lost many things after his diagnosis, including The Juilliard School, but he never lost his gift and love of music. His story became a book, movie, and the subject of many news stories. Seemingly overnight, Jennifer went from being grassroots, mental health advocate, to a consultant on a Hollywood movie, being interviewed by *60 Minutes*, and a national keynote speaker for mental health.

Jennifer's education as a Behavioral Scientist and personal experiences led her to create the Friends of Ayers Foundation (FOA) and the podcast, *Hear the Music. Conversations With*. FOA supplies innovative support through the arts to those suffering from mental health conditions. In Jennifer's podcast, *Hear the Music.*

Conversations With, she creates a platform for her guests to share stories about how mental health challenges have affected them and their families. Jennifer is passionate about raising public awareness that people like Nathaniel face excruciating challenges, discriminating stigma, and a dangerous lack of resources. She knows that a caregiver's journey is as harrowing, albeit quite different, and that they need support, too.

Jennifer hopes her advocacy and call to action will encourage everyone to "Hear the Music" of the mental health community, ignite desire to join her to "STOP STiGMA" associated with mental illness, and vastly improve resources for the mental health community.

Jennifer, an avid golfer, enjoys making and repairing golf clubs. She is a 1973 graduate of John Hay High School. She is also an alumna of Kent State University and National Louis University. Jennifer is a proud member of Alpha Kappa Alpha Sorority, Inc.

www.tracynicole.org

Made in the USA
Columbia, SC
02 May 2021